Sara Saba The Astynomoi Law from Pergamon. A New Commentary

Herausgegeben von

Martin Zimmermann

Die hellenistische Polis als Lebensform BAND 6

Sara Saba

The Astynomoi Law from Pergamon

A NEW COMMENTARY

Verlag Antike

Gedruckt mit freundlicher Unterstützung der Deutschen Forschungsgemeinschaft.

Bibliografische Information der Deutschen Nationalbibliothek
Die Deutsche Nationalbibliothek verzeichnet diese Publikation in der Deutschen Nationalbibliografie; detaillierte bibliografische Daten sind im Internet über http://dnb.d-nb.de abrufbar.

Satz Stylianos Chronopoulos für Verlag Antike
Einbandgestaltung disegno visuelle kommunikation, Wuppertal
Einbandmotive Vorderseite: Modelle von Knidos mit freundlicher Genehmigung von H. Bankel, V. Hinz und S. Franz. Rückseite: Athen, Akropolis. Basis eines Weihgeschenks des Hegelochos. Zeichnung von A. Brauchle und Z. Spyranti mit freundlicher Genehmigung. (Hauptmotiv spiegelverkehrt verwendet; alle Abbildungen in Band 1 dieser Reihe, Stadtbilder im Hellenismus, S. 114, 115 und 226).
Druck und Bindung AZ Druck und Datentechnik GmbH, Kempten
Gedruckt auf säurefreiem und alterungsbeständigem Papier
Printed in Germany

ISBN 978-3-938032-53-4

www.verlag-antike.de

to my parents

Table of Contents

Acknowledgments

This monograph originates from my 2006 PhD dissertation at Duke University, but by now only a little more than the topic itself has survived from that first piece of work.

My main aim in this brief monograph is to provide a new analysis and comment on a unique epigraphic text, namely the so-called Astynomoi Law from Pergamon, which had been edited and commented on in its entirety for the last time by Günther Klaffenbach in 1953/4. A fresh commentary is called for and this I try to complete with the analysis of all available evidence on *astynomoi* from the Greek world.

I am greatly indebted to my advisor, Kent Rigsby, who has followed (patiently) not only my dissertation but also the revision process that has lasted all these years. I also wish to express my thanks to the rest of my dissertation committee and the faculty of the Classics Department in Durham I thank for helping me greatly during my years at Duke.

A special thankyou goes to PD Dr. Helmut Müller who read and commented on the entire manuscript with his usual *akribeia*, generously sharing his unmatched knowledge on Pergamon and its institutions. Also to Dr. Kaja Harter-Uibopuu who provided me with extremely helpful comments on the most –and indeed less– difficult problems in the legal field that emerge in this complex text. Professor Johannes Nollé and PD Dr. Christof Schuler of the Kommission für alte Geschichte und Epigraphik of Munich have consistently helped, encouraged and supported me starting from the time of my Jacoby Stipendium in Munich in 2005 until now.

Finally, I wish to thank Professor Martin Zimmermann for accepting my manuscript in the series "Die hellenistische Polis als Lebensform", Professor Felix Pirson, Director of the DAI Istanbul for all his help, Dr. Martina Erdmann for her very efficient and professional work and Mrs. Harriet Hasenclever who edited my somewhat pidgin English.

Of course I thank also all those family members and friends who tolerated my monomania and suffered patiently listening to my lengthy monologues on this one topic of the Astynomoi Law.

Munich, November 2012 Sara Saba

1 Introduction

In 1901 during the yearly campaign of the German Archeological Institute in Pergamon, the inscription that scholars will know as the 'Astynomoi law' came to light. This is a unique, detailed document that provides insights into the everyday life of a *polis,* Pergamon. In it the duties of the magistrates known as *astynomoi* who were in charge of the administration and maintenance of local infrastructures are made public, accompanied by a detailing of the necessary punishments for possible offenders.

More than a century has gone by since the inscription was found. During this time the excavations have continued almost without interruption and the knowledge on the city, the Attalid institutions and this Royal family's *modus regendi* has grown considerably in the scholarly community. The study of this law, however, after a few years of intense activity,[1] came, as it were, to a standstill after 1954, when Günther Klaffenbach published his excellent edition and commentary on the text.[2] Consequently the writing of another philological commentary was never my intention. The goals of this contribution are of different nature: firstly, I aim to provide an up-to-date study of the epigraphic document in which textual and archaeological evidence, especially that which has emerged since the 1950s, complement each other and help answer questions pertaining to the daily administration of the *polis.* Secondly, given that Hellenistic institutions are now much better understood, I wish to correct or update older views on the offices that the law cites, starting with *astynomia.* This office was not unique to Pergamon, but common to many cities among which that of Athens stands out. This has led scholarship to make of the Athenian *astynomia* the template for this office in general; it is indeed not unusual to see evidence from other communities being interpreted on the basis of the Athenian office. More detrimentally, non-Athenian material is sometimes automatically restored and supplemented with information that comes from Athens alone. Given

---

1 *Ed. princeps* KOLBE 1902; review and comments by LECRIVAIN 1903, on the subsequent improvements to the text see *infra.*

2 KLAFFENBACH 1954, pp. 3–25, reviewed by LAUFFER 1956, pp. 430–431; WOODHEAD 1956, pp. 79–80; BINGEN 1955, pp. 254–255; J. and L. ROBERT *BE* 1955, n. 188.

the general approach of my work, I needed to check the reliability of this view and ask whether the available evidence on *astynomoi* can justify this practice or not. In order to test this widespread approach, in the second part of this monograph I have collected and analyzed all existing data on *astynomoi* in the Greek world. This material seems to indicate that despite the existence of a common pattern in the *astynomoi*'s duties, the representatives of this office did not always have the same role and standing in every city. Unsurprisingly, the evidence does not provide conclusive answers on their institutional role everywhere but the general picture suggests that homonymy does not mean complete homogeneity. Their role in the different cities instead depended on the general institutional setting and on other, more concrete, factors such as the size of a community, for example.

This work took me to Bergama, where ancient Pergamon was located, to see the site and the stone, now on exhibition at the renovated local Museum, and to Munich to read the squeeze that Klaffenbach himself used.[3] The squeeze offers no surprise; the engraved text is clear and, except for lacunae, easily readable. Klaffenbach's edition was based on it and is absolutely authoritative, but I have still found it necessary to provide the text here in which I have recorded as appropriate the improvements that have been suggested over the decades. Also, I include a translation the goal of which is to clarify as far as possible points that might be difficult to understand. I must stress, however, that it has no literary ambition.

---

3 This belongs to the *IG* Archives in Berlin, but is stored at the Kommission für alte Geschichte und Epigraphik in Munich.

2 History of the Studies, Chronology and the Purpose of the Law

In 1902 Kolbe published an *editio princeps* that was completed by a short, essential commentary on the text. This was partly flawed by a few mistakes, but the rapidity with which the text was made available to all well compensated for these inaccuracies, which were most probably due to haste.[4] Moreover, Kolbe was able to establish the double date of the document correctly, namely 2nd century B. C. for the law and 2nd century A. D. for the stone, even if he was for a long time denied the recognition for this accomplishment and even criticized for it. His observation on the imperial re-inscription relied on accurate palaeographical considerations that rested on close *comparanda.* The 1901 campaign was indeed very fruitful: together with the Astynomoi law another inscription came to light, which is now in *OGIS,* 484. This is a letter, possibly by Hadrian, on the abuses in the public banking system that we can securely date to the 2nd century A. D.[5] More importantly, its lettering is practically identical to that of the Astynomoi law to the point that in *OGIS* Dittenberger stated: *ab eodem quadratario incisus videtur titulus n. 484*. For example, both texts preserve characteristic letters of different height, among which φ and ψ stand out as being always larger than all other characters. While the palaeographical analysis strongly supports the 2nd century A. D. for the stone, internal data, such as the name of the month *Pantheios*, L. 205, and several magistrates' titles, prominent among them the *amphodarches* and the *epi tes poleos*, endorses a Hellenistic date for the content.

In the early 20th century, scholars were mostly preoccupied with the edition; this newly published text indeed attracted the attention of the scholarly community, which set out to work to improve Kolbe's edition. The first results appeared already in 1904 by B. Keil who corrected Kolbe's text in several points.[6] Curiously, his remarks went unnoticed at first. Even Dittenberger printed the inscription as n. 483 in the *OGIS*

---

4 See Kolbe 1902, pp. 47–77, Lecrivain 1903's review contained already illuminating comments.

5 *OGIS* 484 dates to around A. D. 129, see Oliver 1989, esp. pp. 208–215, n. 84 who suggests Hadrian's authorship with a question mark. Another term of comparison for the palaeography of the Astynomoi law is *OGIS* 486, on which see *infra* and *AvP* VIII.3.161 with Wörrle's commentary1969, esp. pp. 169–170.

6 See Keil 1904, pp. 73–78.

leaving Kolbe's text unchanged, although in his *addenda et corrigenda* he added several of Keil's corrections.[7] The extraordinary character of the law made it also the object of comparativist studies. For example, in 1907, H. Legras used it as parallel for the Tabula of Herakleia, but still ignored Keil's important textual corrections when he printed the text.[8] It is a curious fact that while Kolbe's correct dating was not accepted, his inaccurate text was quite long-lived and was cited, mostly unchanged, for decades until Klaffenbach's commentary finally appeared in 1954. It represented a watershed in the history of the studies of the Astynomoi law: with the improved edition this scholar changed the way in which the law was understood. His essentially philological commentary addressed the lack of a comprehensive and systematic study on the text. Also, philological contribution aside, Klaffenbach quietly and authoritatively put an end to the discussion that was then raging over the chronology. In 1951, J. H. Oliver had rejected Kolbe's hypothesis to state that both inscription and law belonged to the imperial period. He based this theory on controversial parallels that questioned the assumption made in regard to L. 1 that a Roman emperor could not be called *basileus*.[9] Oliver's theory, but regrettably also Kolbe's, found fierce opponents in J. and L. Robert who thought that both document and stone were late Hellenistic.[10] Their theory relied on the content and internal data, but they also mistakenly judged the palaeography to be late Hellenistic thus neglecting the available comparanda. It was only with Klaffenbach's revision of the evidence that these mistakes were rectified, even if objectively he only restated Kolbe's arguments on the palaeography and internal references that I have already briefly summarized and will be the object of further attention within the commentary. In 1954, Klaffenbach concluded compellingly that stone and content could not date to the same century; instead a double date had to be supported.

---

7 *Addenda et corrigenda*, p. 551.

8 LEGRAS 1907. For the *Tabula Heracleensis* see now the edition and commentary in CRAWFORD (ed.) *Roman Statutes* vol. II, n. 24, 1996. GIOVANNINI 2008, pp. 47–61 offers a guide to the latest developments of modern research on the text with a different interpretation than Crawford's, esp. p. 48.

9 In L. 1 of the document the law is called *basiliko(s)*, which for Oliver qualified the authority passing the document.

10 See OLIVER 1951, esp. pp. 200–201 and J. and L. ROBERT *BE* 1952, n. 137.

Incidentally, all opponents of this dating reviewed their statements and agreed with the double chronology,[11] which is now universally accepted.

Today it is virtually certain that the law was originally passed during the Attalid period in the 2nd century B. C., according to some possibly under Eumenes II. This king is known to have promoted a building program that aimed to add new areas to the city and that a stricter regulation of the administration and maintenance of (old and new) public infrastructures must have followed or accompanied.[12] Speculation aside, we do not have any direct confirmation of this theory. As a matter of course, if Müller and Wörrle's tentative hypothesis for which the official named *epi ton hieron prosodon* was not introduced in the Attalid administration until the time of Attalos II or even Attalos III is right, then this *prostagma* could not have been enacted till the last decades of the Attalid rule.[13]

Later, in fact almost 3 centuries afterward, in the 2nd century A. D., the text was re-inscribed, be that under Trajan or Hadrian. Curiously, this is a point that scholarship has hardly debated for it prefers Hadrian, even if solid evidence for this is lacking.[14] The accuracy of this view and its basis, along with its repercussions, I discuss in the commentary, but a few words on its genesis and prevalence can illuminate some aspects of the reception of the text.

In the *editio princeps*, Kolbe suggested that the law had been reinscribed under Trajan because[15] "(es) dem Schriftcharakter nach mit den Denkmälern des C. Antius Aulus Quadratus übereinstimmt (und

---

11 See OLIVER 1955, pp. 88–92 and J. and L. ROBERT *BE* 1955, n. 188.

12 See STRAB. XIII.4.2 = 624 C, on which see VIRGILIO 1984, pp. 24–37. KLAFFENBACH 1954, but also in 1958, p. 24 seems to suggest that this law had been passed under Eumenes, OLIVER 1955, p. 88 ended up agreeing with him and so did the ROBERTS *BE* 1955, n. 188.

13 For the *epi ton hieron prosodon* see my comment on LL. 176–180 with bibliographical references; MÜLLER – WÖRRLE 2002, pp. 231–232, esp. n. 194. ALLEN 1971, p. 171, and before him CORRADI 1929, p. 390, or even LECRIVAIN 1903, already said that this law could date to a time after Eumenes' reign. For example Allen said: "The original law dates from a time when the city was fully developed, that is during the reign of Eumenes II or possibly Attalos II or III – in any event after the treaty of Apameia". Still, all these scholars, even if they showed the necessary caution, seemed partial to Eumenes II.

14 See VIRGILIO 1993, pp. 110–114.

15 See KOLBE 1902, p. 55.

dadurch etwa in die Zeit Trajans verwiesen wird)"[16] The palaeographic argument is the strongest for the imperial dating of the stone, but cannot be considered definite proof for a more precise chronology. In the section devoted to the dating, Klaffenbach first concluded that for the inscription "die Datierung in den Anfang des 2. Jahrh. n. Ch., *mag es nun trajanische oder bereits hadrianische Zeit sein* (italics mine) muss beibehalten werden"[17] which suggests that he did not intend to take a firm stand on the issue. Later in his work, however, he returned to this point to specify his preference for the Hadrianic period because: "das ist die Zeit des Archaismus, der mit Hadrian die grosse Mode geworden ist."[18] I must note too that this corresponds with his general opinion on the document and its value, which makes this comment somewhat biased. Oliver too inclined toward a year under Hadrian, even after he recanted his 1951 opinion on chronology in general. Certainly, his attitude further favored the spreading of this idea.[19]

In this contribution the double date is accepted without reservations, but I do not intend to take a definite stand on the matter of the king and the emperor under whom the inscription was engraved. Occasional remarks on chronology and hypotheses on the most likely circumstances for both the passing and reinscribing of the law will appear throughout the commentary. This is a persistent theme because it has repercussions on the second important issue pertaining to this law, namely its significance and role in the 2nd century A. D. The question of why it had

16 *OGIS* 486, on this dossier Müller 2009, pp. 367–368 and appendix.

17 Klaffenbach 1954, p. 21 defended Kolbe from the attacks brought forward by Oliver 1951 and the Robert(s) in 1952.

18 Klaffenbach 1954, p. 24. On the antiquarian interests of society in the 2nd century A. D. see Andrei 1984, who through an analysis of Claudius Charax's fragments gives a lucid portrait of the spirit that animated this century and its will to recover the past.

19 Mine is a call for caution, but signs are there that allow a preference for Hadrian over Trajan. In general, we know that in the 2nd century A. D. Pergamon flourished again and to some extent Hadrian played a part. Virgilio 1993, pp. 111–114 suggests that by bringing back the city to its past splendor, Hadrian may have aimed to increase his popularity. In other words he tried to associate himself with the beloved Eumenes II. Boatwright 2000, esp. her reflections on p. 13, has shown that Hadrian was keen on rediscovering the past and local history, to the restoration of which he often directed his interventions. On Hadrian's activities and initiatives see Halfmann 2001, pp. 55–63 and the recent contribution by Müller, 2009, pp. 368–406 on Hadrian and Pergamon.

been re-inscribed cannot be avoided here. In 1954 Klaffenbach took a controversial stand on this point by opposing the widespread opinion which assumed that the law had been re-inscribed because it was still applicable. He denied any practical purpose to it and hypothesized that the stone was a summa honoraria that somebody dedicated when entering the office of *astynomia*, in spite of the fact that its content was no longer applicable. In brief, it was a *monumentum*.[20] The prescript, which clarifies the dedicatory nature of the document, cannot alone overrule this suggestion since it reveals that it was not public money that paid for it. A citizen could do what he wanted with his money after all. At the same time, however, the same initial line does not invalidate the theory of the applicability of the law. Since the dedicatee was about to enter *astynomia,* he might have wanted to broadcast his future duties through a Hellenistic – but still applicable – law. The acceptance of this interpretation presupposes a degree of continuity through the centuries. Sources testify to the existence of *astynomoi* in the 2nd century A. D. and later too. It is undeniable that under Roman rule magistrates that were long known in Greek *poleis* continued to exist. A case in point, under Commodus Ankara has *astynomoi* of whose duties, however, we know nothing. Nonetheless, Bosch assumed that these were comparable to the Athenian *astynomoi* who operated already in the 5th–4th B. C.[21] Even if daring, and to some extend debatable, Bosch's statement cannot and should not be criticized without further qualification. It is very likely that the basic tasks of this type of magistrates did not change drastically over time, but one must always consider a city's location and size before making comparisons for example. Still scholarship is prone to generalization and a passage from the Digest, possibly an extract from an ἀστυνομικὸς μονόβιβλος by Papinian, *D.* 43.10, has encouraged this attitude by attesting to responsibilities of *astynomoi* that seem very close to those known for the Hellenistic magistrates, at least in Pergamon. In this regard, Hennig commented: "Wie der D. 43.10.21 zitierte Auszug aus dem in griechischer Sprache verfaßten ἀστυνομικὸς μονόβιβλος Papinians zeigt, hatte sich, wie nicht anders zu erwarten, in severischer Zeit in diesem Bereich nichts Grundsätzliches geändert."[22] Urban policing duties,

20 Klaffenbach 1954, pp. 24–25.
21 Bosch 1967, pp. 262–264.
22 Hennig 1995, esp. p. 236.

i. e. a city's daily administration, must have been similar (but certainly not identical) over time in communities of comparable size, which is also why it should not be too problematic to accept that the Astynomoi law was still applicable in the 2nd century A. D. in Pergamon. An entering *astynomos* thought it was appropriate to show the citizenry the duties he was about to take upon himself and the efforts his office required by a Hellenistic regulation that must still have been in use. This, however, does not mean that one can forget chronology and geography and ascribe to all *astynomoi* the same tasks and role.

The debate on the significance of this text has not yet reached any conclusion and Klaffenbach's idea of a *monumentum* has found both followers and critics. Scholarship indeed supports two different and contrasting theses: *(a)* the law was a Hellenistic document re-inscribed for its historical and symbolic value without any practical purpose; *(b)* the law was still applicable and for this reason was engraved anew.[23] This thorny problem may never find a solution, but a new analysis of the evidence and a discussion on both theories form a part of the present commentary, which, however, definitely tends to support the applicability thesis. The document represented a city regulation designed to meet the daily needs of a community, which hardly changed through the centuries. Communities needed a building policy, administration of water resources and the like; basic needs, especially when confined to the same community, defy time.

[23] See my conclusions *infra*. It must be stressed, however, that most scholars believe that the law was still applicable in the 2nd century A. D., for example VIRGILIO 1993, pp. 110–114; the ROBERTS in *BE* 1955, n. 188;BINGEN 1955, pp. 244–255.

3 Edition and Translation of the Astynomoi Law

Plaque of white marble with grayish-blue stripes that consists of 12 adjoining fragments. In the photograph that Klaffenbach provided a thirteenth fragment is in place (Fig. 1, see p. 148), but appears to be lost today. The upper left part of the plaque is broken with a loss of the first 33 lines circa for column I and 15 lines in column II. The bottom part of the whole stele is also damaged and an undetermined number of lines are missing at the end of each column. H. 0.82; L. 1.05; Th. 0.05–0.08. Letters: 0.005–0.012 (heading).

The stone was found in the Lower Market of Pergamon in 1901 during the excavation by the German Archeological Institute (Fig. 2, see p. 149). Today the inscription is on display in the Bergama Museum. The squeeze used by Klaffenbach belongs to the *IG* Archives, but is currently stored at the Kommission für Alte Geschichte und Epigraphik in Munich.

Edd: *editio princeps* Kolbe, *AM* 27, 1902, pp. 46–55; (Legras, *La table latine* 1907, pp. 373–382; Dittenberger, *OGIS* 483); Klaffenbach *(M)DAI* 1954, pp. 4 – 8 (squeeze; ph.); (*SEG* XIII 521); (Saliou, *Les lois*, 1994, pp. 191–198; Hellmann, *Choix d'inscriptions*, 1999, n. 2, pp. 13–22; Chandezon, *L'élevage en Grèce*, 2003, pp. 188–196, LL. 188–202). Collation, 2004.

Cf. Keil, *AM* 29, 1904, pp. 75–78 with improvements to the text; Hitzig, *ZeitSavStift. Rom. Abt.* 26, 1905, pp. 432–447 and 483 devoted to the problem of the confiscation of slave-master's property; J. and L. Robert, *BE* 61, 1948, n. 172; 65, 1952, n. 11 and 137; 69, 1956, n. 243 on the chronology and philological problems of text; Seyfarth, *Aegyptus* 35, 1955, pp. 29–31 on the *agora plethouse*; Oliver, *Hesperia* 24, 1955, pp. 88–92 on chronology; Lauffer, *HistZeit* 181, 1956, pp. 430–431 on the first line; Klaffenbach 1958, pp. 24–25 on his own restorations; Hennig 1995, pp. 249–250 new restoration of L. 32 and comment.

3.1 Edition

- - - - - - -]Σ ἀστυνομῶν τὸν βασιλικὸν νόμον ἐκ τῶν ἰδίων ἀνέθηκεν

Col. I

[- - ἐπισκοπείτωσαν καὶ ἐπικρεινέτ]ω-
[σαν, καθ' ἃ ἂν αὐτοῖς φαίνητα]ι̣ δίχ̣αιον
[εἶναι. καὶ ἐὰν] μηδ' οὕτως πείθωνται,
[οἱ μὲν] στρατηγοὶ ζημιώσαντες αὐτοὺς
[τῆ]ι̣ ἐκ τοῦ νόμου ζημίαι παραδότωσαν
τῶι πράκτορι πράσσειν. οἱ δὲ ἀστυνόμοι
ἔκδοσιν ποιησάμενοι τῆς ἀποκαταστά-
σεως{εως} τοῦ τόπου εἰς τὰ ἐξ ἀρχῆς ἐ-
ν ἡμέραις δέκα, τὸ διάφορον πράξαν-
τες ἡμιόλιον παρὰ τῶν ἀπειθούντων
ἀποκαταστησάτωσαν τοῖς μὲν ἠργο-
λαβηκόσιν τὸ ἐπιβάλλον, τὸ δὲ λοιπὸν
τοῖς ταμίαις. ἐὰν δὲ μὴ ποιήσωσιν οἱ
ἀστυνόμοι, καθάπερ ὁ νόμος προστάσ-
σει, τὴν μὲν ἔκδοσιν ποιείσθωσαν οἱ
στρατηγοί, τὸ δὲ λοιπὸν διάφορον τῆς
ἐκδόσεως πραχθήτωσαν οἱ ἀστυνό-
μοι καὶ ἐκτὸς ἀποτεινέτωσαν ζημί-
ας δραχμὰς ἑκατόν. πραξάτωσαν δὲ
αὐτοὺς οἱ νομοφύλακες παραχρῆμα.
κατὰ ταὐτὰ δὲ γεινέσθω καὶ ἐπὶ τῶν
ἄλλων τῶν ἀπειθούντων. ἔστωσαν
δὲ τῶν κατὰ τὴν χώραν ὁδῶν αἱ μὲν
λεωφόροι μὴ ἐλάσσους τὸ πλάτος πη-
χῶν εἴκοσιν, αἱ δὲ ἄλλαι μὴ ἐλάσσους
πηχῶν ὀκτώ, ἐὰν μή τινες κατὰ τὰς >
γειτνιάσεις ἕνεκεν τῆς πρὸς ἀλλήλους
διόδου ἀτραποῖς χρῶνται. παρεχέσθωσαν
δὲ καθαρὰς καὶ πορευσίμους τὰς ὁδοὺς
[οἱ τ]ὰ κτήματα κεκτημένοι παρὰ τὰς ὁ-
[δοὺς κατὰ] τὴν γειτνίασιν ἕως σταδίων
[. . $^{2 \text{ or } 3}$. συνει]σφέροντες καὶ συνεπισκευ-
[άζοντες. καὶ] ἐὰν ἀπε[ιθῶσιν, ἐν]εχυραζέτ[ω]-

[σαν αὐτοὺς οἱ - - - - - - - - - - -]
[- - - - - - - - - - - - - - - - - - -]

Col. II

. . . . .ΩΝΗ
. . . . ΩΝΑ
. . . . ΕΥΜΕ̣
. . . . ΤΗΙ
. . . . ΕΝΟΥ
. . . . ΥΠΑ
. . . . ΑΡ
. . . . ΙΕΣ
. . . . .Υ
. . . . Π̣ΑΡ
. . . .
. . . . ΣΡΑ. .
[- - - - - - - - - - - - - τοὺς δ' ἐ]κβεβλη-
[κότας ---$^{c.6}$---- οἱ ἀμφοδάρχα]ι̣ ἀναγκα-
[ζέτωσαν ἀνακαθαίρειν τὸν τ]όπον, καθ' ἃ
[ὁ νόμος προστάσσει. εἰ δὲ μ]ή, προσαγγελ-
[λέτωσαν τοῖς ἀστυνόμοις.] οἱ δὲ ἀστυνό-
[μοι ἐκδότωσαν μετὰ τοῦ ἀ]μφοδάρχου καὶ
[τὸ γενόμενον ἀνάλωμα] πραξάτωσαν
[τοὺς ἀπειθοῦντας παραχρ]ῆμα καὶ ζημι-
[ούτωσαν δραχμαῖς . . . . ἐ]ὰ̣ν̣ δέ τις τῶν ἀμ-
[φοδαρχῶν μὴ ποιήσηι τι τ]ῶν προγεγραμμέ-
[νων, ζημιούσθω ὑπὸ τ]ῶν ἀστυνόμων κα-
[θ' ἕκαστον ἀτάκτημα δ]ραχμαῖς εἴκοσιν. τὰ
[δὲ γεινόμενα δ]ιάφορα ἐκ τῶν ἐπιτί-
[μων ἀποδιδόσθω]σαν ἐκ μηνὸς εἰς μῆ-
[να τοῖς ταμίαις κ]αὶ ὑπαρχέ̣τω[σ]α̣ν, ἐὰν
[χρεία γείνηται (?)], εἰς τὴν ἀνακάθαρσ[ι]ν
[τῶν τόπων, εἰ]ς δὲ ἄλλο μηθὲν μεταναφε-
[ρέσθω. τῆ]ς δὲ πράξεως καὶ τῶν ἄλλων
[πάντ]ων ἐπιμε[λ]είσθωσαν οἱ ἀστυνόμοι.
[ἐὰ]ν̣ δέ τι μὴ ποιήσωσιν οὗτοι τῶν γεγραμ-

μένων, ζημιούσθωσαν ὑπὸ τῶν στρατη-
γῶν καὶ τοῦ ἐπὶ τῆς πόλεως καθ᾽ ἕκαστον
ἀτάκτημα δραχμαῖς πεντήκοντα καὶ κα-
τατασσέσθω καὶ αὕτη ἡ ζημία εἰς τὰ προγε-
γραμμένα. *vvv* χοός *vvv* ἐάν τινες ἐν̣ ταῖς
ὁδοῖς χοῦν ὀρύσσωσιν ἢ λίθους ἢ πηλὸν ποι-
ῶσιν ἢ πλίνθους ἕλκωσιν ἢ μετεώρους
ὀχετοὺς ποιῶσιν, κωλυέτωσαν αὐτοὺς
οἱ ἀμφοδάρχαι. ἐὰν δὲ μὴ πείθωνται, ἐ[[σ]]-
παν<γ>ελλέτωσαν τοῖς ἀστυνόμοις. οὗτοι
δὲ ζημιούτωσαν τὸν ἀπειθοῦντα καθ′ ἕ-
καστον ἀτάκτημα δραχμαῖς πέντε καὶ
ἀναγκαζέτωσαν τά τε ἄλλα ἀποκαθιστά-
ναι εἰς τὰ ἐξ ἀρχῆς καὶ τοὺς ὀχετοὺς κρυ-
πτοὺς ποιεῖν. ἐὰν δὲ μηδ′ οὕτω πειθαρχῶ-
σιν οἱ ἰδιῶται, ἔκδοσιν ποιείσθωσαν ἐν ἡ-
μέραις δέκα καὶ τὸ γενόμενον ἀνάλωμα
πραξάτωσαν παρὰ τῶν ἀπειθούντων ἡμιό-
λιον. ὁμοίως δὲ καὶ τοὺς προϋπάρχοντας ὀχε-
τοὺς ἐπαναγκαζέτωσαν κρυπτοὺς ποι-
εῖν. ἐὰν δέ τι τούτων μὴ ποιήσωσιν οἱ ἀ-
στυνόμοι, αὐτοὶ ἔνοχοι ἔστωσαν ταῖς ἴσαις
ζημίαις. *vvvvv* πράξεως *vvvv* ἐάν τινες
μὴ ἀποδιδῶσιν τῶν κοινῇ ἀνακαθαρθ<έ>ν-
των ἀμφόδων τὸ γεινόμενον μέρος τῆς
ἐκδόσεως τῶν κοπρίων ἢ τῶν ἐπιτίμων,
λαμβανέτωσαν αὐτῶν οἱ ἀμφοδάρχαι
ἐνέχυρα καὶ τιθέσθωσαν ἐνεχυρασίαν
πρὸς τοὺς ἀστυνόμους αὐθημερὸν ἢ τῆι ὑ-
στεραίαι καί, ἐὰν μηθεὶς ἐξομόσηται τὰ ἐ-
νεχυρασθέντα ἐν ἡμέραις πέντε, πωλεί-
τωσαν αὐτὰ ἢ ἐν φράτρηι ἢ ἐν τῆι ἀγορᾷ πλη-
θυούσῃ συνπαρόντων τῶν ἀστυνόμων
καὶ τὸ μὲν γεινόμενον κομι<ζ>έσθωσαν
. . . . ἀπ̣ο̣. . .ΟΣΜ̣. . . .

Col. III

ἐπισκοπείτωσα[ν κ]αί, ἐὰν φαίνωντα[ι] αὐτοῖς ἐπισκευά[σι]μοι εἶναι, ἐπισκευαζέτωσαν οἱ κεκτημένοι. ἐὰν δέ τινες αὐτῶν μὴ βούλωνται, ἐκδότωσαν οἱ ἀστυνόμοι μετὰ τοῦ προαιρουμένου τῶν βλαπτομένων. τοῦ δὲ γενομένο[υ ἀ]ναλώματος πραξάτωσαν παραχρῆμα παρὰ μὲν τοῦ ἀπειθοῦντος τὰ τρία μέρη, παρὰ δὲ τοῦ ἄλλου τὰ δύο καὶ ἀποκα[τ]αστησάτωσαν τοῖς ἠργολαβηκόσι[ν]. τῶν δὲ δεομένων ἐπισκευῆς κοινῶ[ν] τοίχων ἢ καταπεσόντων, ἐὰν μὲν ὅλοις τοῖς τοίχοις ὁμοίως οἱ γείτονες χρῶνται, τὸ ἴσον εἰσφ[ε]ρέτωσαν εἰς τὴν οἰκοδομίαν. ἐὰν δὲ ὁ μ̣ὲ̣ν προσοικῇ πρὸς τῶι τοίχωι, ὁ δὲ ὑπα[ίθ]ρωι χρῆται, εἰσφερ̣έτωσαν εἰς τὴ[ν] οἰκοδομίαν ὁ μὲν προσοικῶν τὰ δύο μέρη, ὁ δὲ ὑπαίθρῳ χρώμενος τὸ τρίτον. ὁμοίως δὲ ἀποτινέτωσαν καὶ ἐὰν ὁ μὲν ὑπερῶιον οἴκημα πρὸς αὐτῶι ἔχῃ, ὁ [δ]ὲ ἁπλοῦν. ἔστω δὲ περὶ μὲν τ<ῶ>ν κοινῶν τοίχων ὑπὲρ τοῦ καταφθείροντος πρόσκλησις πρὸς τοὺς ἀστυνόμους καί, ἐὰν φαίν<ω>νται ἔνοχοι ὄντες κρίσει νικηθέντες, ἀποτινέτωσαν τὴν βλάβην αὐτῶν. μὴ ἐξουσία δὲ ἔστω ἐπὶ τοὺς κοινοὺς τοίχους μήτε ἐποικοδομεῖν μήτε διορύσσειν μήτε ἄλλο καταβλάπτειν μηθέν, ἐὰν μὴ πείσωσιν το[ὺς] κυρίους. ὅσοι δὲ τοῖχοι π̣ρ̣όσχωροι ὄντ̣ες [β]λ̣άπτουσιν τοὺς ἐνοικοῦντας, ἐὰν βούλω[ν]ται αὐτοῖς οἱ κύριοι ὑπαίθροις οὖσιν τὰ πρὸς τοὺς γείτονας περιστάσεις ποιεῖν, μηθὲν βλάπτοντες τοὺς γείτονας μὴ κωλυέ[σθωσα]ν πο[ι]εῖν τὸ πλάτος μὴ πλεῖον πήχε̣ω̣ς καὶ στεγάζοντες αὐτὰς παραχρῆ-

μα γείσεσιν λιθίνοις, τοῦ ἐκτὸς τοίχου τῆς περιστάσεως οἰκοδομηθέντος ἀσφαλῶς, ἐὰν μὴ πέτρα{ι} ᾖ, οὗ τὰ γείση ἐπιτεθήσεται. μὴ ποιείτωσαν δὲ στεγά[ζον]τες ὑψηλότερον τὸ ἔδαφος τοῦ λοιποῦ ὑπαίθρου πλὴν ὅσον ὕδατι ἀπόρρουν. κύριοι δὲ ἔστωσαν τῶν μὲν περιστάσεων οἱ ποιήσαντες, τῶν δὲ ἐπ' αὐτῶν τόπων, ὅταν στεγασθῶσιν, οἱ γείτονες εἰς μηθὲν χρώμενοι, ἐξ οὗ καταβλάψουσιν τοὺς ἀλλοτρίους τοίχους. ποιείτωσαν δὲ τὰς εἰσόδους τῶν περιστάσεων ἐκ τῶν ἰδίων οἰκιῶν. ἐὰν δὲ ἀδύνατον ᾖ κρείνοντος τοῦ ἀρχιτέκτονος μετὰ τῶν ἀστυνόμων, διδότωσαν οἱ γείτονες τὴν εἴσοδον τοῖς εἰσπορευομένοις ἕνεκεν ἀνακαθάρσε<ω>ς, ὁμοίως δὲ καὶ ἐὰν πτώματος γενομένου ἐπισκευῆς προσδέωνται. ὑπὲρ δὲ τῶν κατ' ἐπηρεασμὸν εἰσπορευομένων ἐπικρείνοντες οἱ ἀστυνόμοι, ἐὰν καταλαμβάνωσιν, ζημιούτωσαν αὐτὸν δραχμαῖς πέντε. μηθεὶς δὲ πρὸς ἀλλοτρίωι ἢ κοινῶι τοίχωι μήτε ὀρύγματα ποιείτω μήτε πιθάκνας ἱστάτωι μήτε φυτευέτωι μήτε ἄλλο ποιείτωι μηθέν, ἐξ οὗ καταβλάψει τ<ὸ>ν τοῖχον. εἰ δὲ μή, ἐὰν ἐνκαλῇ ὁ κύριος, οἱ ἀστυνόμοι ἐπισκοπείτωσαν καὶ ἐπικρεινέτωσαν, καθ' ἃ ἂν αὐτοῖς φαίνηται δίκαιον εἶναι. καὶ ὅσοι δ' ἂν τοῖχοι τῶν ἀλλοτρίων οἰκιῶν μέλλοντες καταπείπτειν, προφ[ηνάν]των <τῶν> γειτόνων τὴν βλάβην - - - -
ρα γεινομέ[ν]η̣ επι . . . Α̣Σ̣ - - - - - - -
- -

Col. IV

καζέτωσαν ἐκκαθαίρειν τοὺς ὑπονόμους. *vvvv* κρηνῶν *vvvvv* περὶ τῶν ἐν τῆι πόλει καὶ τοῖς προαστίοις κρηνῶν ἐπιμελὲς γεινέσθω τοῖς ἀστυνόμοις, ὅπως καθαραί τε ὦσιν καὶ οἱ εἰς αὐτὰς ὑπόνομοι εἰσάγοντες καὶ ἐξάγοντες τὸ [ὕ]δω̣ρ εὔρους ὑπάρχωσιν. ἐὰν δέ τιν<ε>ς ἐπισκ[ε]υῆς προσδέωνται, προσαγγελλέτωσαν τοῖς στρατηγοῖς καὶ τῶι ἐπὶ τῶν ἱερῶν προσόδων, ὅπως διὰ τούτων γείνωνται αἱ ἐκδόσεις. μηθ̣ενὶ δὲ ἐξουσία ἔστω ἐπὶ τῶν δημοσίων κρη̣νῶν μήτε κτῆνος ποτίζειν μήτε ἱμάτια πλύνειν μήτε σκεῦος μήτε ἄλλο ἁπλῶς μηθὲν. ὁ δὲ τούτων τι ποιήσας, ἐὰν μὲν ἐλεύθερος ᾖ, τῶν τε κτηνῶν καὶ ἱματίων καὶ τῶν σκευῶν στερείσθω καὶ αὐτὸς ζημιούσθω δραχμαῖς πεντήκοντα, ἐὰν δὲ οἰκέτης, ἐὰν μὲν μετὰ τῆς τοῦ κυρίου γνώμης ποιήσῃ τι τούτων, ὁμοίως στερέσθω καὶ αὐτὸς μαστιγούσθω ἐν τῶι κύφωνι πληγαῖς πεντήκοντα, ἐὰν δὲ ἄνευ τῆς τοῦ κυρίου γνώμης, ὧν μὲν ἂν ἔχῃ, στερέσθω, μαστειγωθεὶς δὲ ἐν τῶι κύφωνι πληγαῖς ἑκατὸν δεδέσθω ἐν τῶι ξύλωι ἡμέρας δέκα καί, ὅταν ἀφείηται, ἀφειέσθω μαστειγωθεὶς μὴ ἐλά<σ>σοσιν πληγαῖς πεντήκοντα. ἔστω δὲ τ̣ῶ̣ν ἄλ{ι}λων τῶι βουλομένωι ἐπίληψις τῶν κ̣α̣κουργούντων περὶ τὰς κρήνας, καὶ ὁ ἀναγαγὼν ἢ ἀνενέγκας ἐπὶ τοὺς ἀστυνόμους τὰ ληφθέντα μεριζέσθω τοῦ γεινομένου ἐξ αὐτῶν διαφόρου τ̣<ὸ> ἥμισυ, τὰ δὲ λοιπὰ κατατασσέσθω εἰς τὴν ἐπισκευὴν τοῦ τῶν Νυμφῶν ἱεροῦ.

vv φρεάτ{ρ}ων *vv* οἱ καθεσταμένοι ἀστυνόμοι τὰς ὑπαρχούσας ἐν ταῖς οἰκίαις δεξαμεν[ὰ]ς ἀναγραφόμενοι ἐν τῶι Πανθείωι μηνὶ τιθέσθωσαν τὴν γραφὴν πρὸς τοὺς στρατηγοὺς καὶ ἐπιμελείσθωσαν, ἵνα οἱ κύριοι στεγνὰς παρέχωνται καὶ μηδεμία τῶν προϋπαρχουσῶν ἐνχωννύηται. εἰ δὲ μή, τοὺς τούτων τι ποιοῦντας ζημιώσαντες καθ᾽ ἑκάστην δεξαμενὴν δραχμαῖς ἑκατὸν πραξάτωσαν [καὶ ἀνα]γκαζέτωσαν ἐκκαθᾶραι. καὶ εἴ τινες δὲ πρ̣ότερον ἐνκεχωσμέναι εἰσίν, παραγγελλέτωσαν τοῖς κυρίοις, ὅπως ἐκκαθαίρωσιν ἐν μησὶν ὀκτώι. ἐὰν δὲ μὴ ποιήσωσι, πράξαντες καὶ τούτο̣υ̣ς τὴν αὐτὴν ζημίαν ἐπαναγκαζέτωσαν ἐκκαθαίρειν. τὰ δὲ γεινόμενα διάφορα τῶν ζημιῶν ἀποδιδόσθωσαν ἐκ μηνὸς εἰς μῆνα τοῖς ταμίαις καὶ ὑπαρχέτωσαν εἰς τὴν ἀνακάθαρσιν καὶ κατασκευὴν τῶν δεξαμενῶν, εἰς δὲ ἄλλο μηθὲν μεταφερέσθω. ὅσοι δ᾽ ἂν φρέατα κεκτημένοι μὴ π[οιοῦ]ντες στεγνὰ βλάπτωσιν τοὺς γείτονας, ἐ[πανα]γκαζέτωσαν αὐτοὺς οἱ ἀστυνόμοι ζημ[ιοῦντες] καί, ἐάν τινες διὰ ταῦτα γείνωνται καταδίκ[αι, πρά]ξαντες οἱ ἀστυνόμοι ἀποδότωσαν τοῖς β[λα]πτομένοις. ὅσοι δ᾽ ἂν τῶν ἀστυνόμων μὴ θῶνται τὴν ἐφ᾽ ἑαυτῶν γραφὴν τῶν φρεάτων εἰς τὸ ἀρχεῖον ἢ μὴ ποιήσωσιν, καθ᾽ ἃ ὁ νόμος προστάσσει, πραξάτωσαν αὐτοὺς οἱ νομοφύλακες δραχμὰς ἑκατὸν καὶ καταταξάτωσαν εἰς τὰς αὐτὰς προσόδους.

v ἀφεδρώνων *v* οἱ ἀστυνόμοι ἐπιμέλειαν ποιείσθωσαν τῶν τε δημοσίων ἀφεδρ[ών]ων καὶ τῶν ἐξ αὐτῶν ὑπονόμων καί, [ὅσοι ἂν μὴ] στεγνοὶ ὑπάρχωσιν καὶ τῶν - - - . . . . αὐτοίς . . . Σ . . . . ΗΡΓ. .. .

Readings of Klaffenbach, restorations of Kolbe. 1 ἀστυνόμων L(egras); Kl(affenbach); ἀστυνομῶν K(olbe); D(ittenberger). 9 ΣΕΩΣΩΕΩΣ lapis, corr. Kl; K. 17 {λοιπὸν} del. Kl., W(oodhead). 19/20 ζημί/α(ν) K. See Wilhelm 1925 defending the reading ζημίας which is on the stone. 22 γεινέσθωσαν καὶ K. and D., γενέσθωσαν L. 26 εἴκοσι K. corr. Keil. 29 παρεχέτωσαν K. 30 καθαρούς K corr. Keil. 31/32 παρὰ τὰς ο(ἰ)/[κίας K; ὁ[δοὺς Keil. 32 ὁ/[δοὺς καὶ] D., Kl. 33 [δέκα] rest. D. 38 ΕΥΜΕ K, Kl. 49 [κότας τὸν χοῦν (?)] K. suggests τὸν κόπρον as alternative restoration. 51 [ἂν ὁ νόμος προστάσσει] Kl. 54 [τὸ διάφορον ἡμιόλιον] D.; 56 δραχμαῖς δέκα] K. 58 Kl.; ζημιούσθωσαν K. 60/1 D., ἐπιτι/μῶν K. 63 [τι προσδέηται] K. 64 ὁδῶν Kl. with question mark, K., D., L. without question mark. 64/65 Kl.; μεταναφε[ρέθωσαν τῆ]ς K. 75/6 ἐ[[σ]]/παν<γ>ελλέτωσαν Σ erased. 77 ΠΑΝΤΕΛΛ lapis 89 ταῖς αὐταῖς K., corr. Kl. 91 ΘΟΝ lapis. 93 τῶν κοπριῶν ἢ τῶν ἐπιτιμῶν K., corr. D. 96/97 ὑ/στερείαι K. 99 ἀγορᾶι K. 101, ΚΟΜΙΣΕ lapis, corr. Keil, D. 113 σμένων L. 123 TON lapis, corr. K. 126 NON lapis, corr. K. 134 τὰ<ς> K. 141 πέτραι Kl., πέτραια K., D., L. 154 EOS lapis, corr. K. 160 ὄρυγμα K. 163 TVN lapis, corr. Kl. 167/8 προφ[ερόντων] τῶν γείτονων K., προφ[ηνάντων] τῶν γειτόνων D. 168/9 [τὰ μὲν διάφο]ρα γεινόμε[να] ΕΠΥ̣ K.; καὶ ὅσα ἔτε]/ρα D.; 170 [ἀναγ]/καζέτωσαν K. 176 εὔ<ρ>ρους K. 177 ΤΙΝΟΣ lapis, τινες K. 195 ἀφείσθω K., corr. Kl. 213 κεχωσμένοι and παραγ K., 224 Kl., ζημ[ίαις] K. 236 ἐὰν τινες σ]τεγνοὶ K., ἐὰν τινες μὴ σ]τεγνοί D., which Kl. judged too long.

3.2 Translation

Prescript

[...] being *astynomos* he dedicated the royal law at his own expense.

Col. I

Let them inspect and take the appropriate decisions following the principles that seem just to them. In case these do not obey (this provision), after fining them with the penalty established by the law the *strategoi* shall leave the collection (of the money) to the *praktor*. (7) After assigning the work to bidders to restore the area to its original condition within ten days, the *astynomoi* who are in charge of collecting the due amount of money increased by half from those who did not comply, shall give their due to the contractors, and the rest to the treasurers. (14) If the *astynomoi* do not do as the law orders, the *strategoi* shall send out the contract, the *astynomoi* shall be charged with the surplus of the restoration cost and pay a fine of 100 drachmas in addition. (20) The *nomophylakes* shall collect from them immediately. Likewise, the same rule shall apply to others who do not comply. (23) Among the roads that run through the countryside, the main suburban roads (*leophoroi*) shall not be less than 20 cubits in width, the other streets not less than eight cubits, unless some use pathways as access to one another through the [different] areas. (29) Those who have properties along the streets in each area at a distance of up to [?] stadia shall keep the streets clean and passable [...] by contributing and repairing them together. If they do not comply the [?] shall confiscate [...]

Col. II

(48) [...] Those who have thrown out [...] the *amphodarchai* shall force (them?) to clean the area, as the law prescribes. Otherwise, they shall report them to the *astynomoi*. (52) The *astynomoi* shall leave the contract with the *amphodarches* and immediately collect the resulting sum from those who do not comply and fine them [...] drachmas. (56) If any one of the *amphodarchai* does not carry out any of the prescribed actions, he is to be fined twenty drachmas for each infraction by the *astynomoi*. (59) The revenues from the penalties shall be given monthly to the treasurers and be available, in case of necessity, for the cleaning of the (civic) areas, and shall not be diverted to another purpose. (65) The *astynomoi* shall take care of the collection and of everything else. If they do not attend to any of their duties, they shall be fined by the *strategoi* and the official in charge of the city 50 drachmas for each misdeed. The fine shall be redirected towards the activities that have been mentioned above. (72) Rubble: if people dig rubble or stones in the streets or make mud or remove bricks or uncover conduits, the *amphodarchai* shall stop them. (76) If they do not comply, they shall report them to the *astynomoi*. These shall fine the transgressor five drachmas for each infraction and force him to restore everything to its previous condition and to cover the conduits. (82) If the residents do not comply, they shall assign the work within ten days and collect the resulting sum plus half from those who disobey. (86) Similarly, they shall force them to cover the already existing conduits. If the *astynomoi* do not do any of these things, they are liable to the same fines. (90) Collection: if any do not give their acquired share of the contract (for the collection) of dung or of the fines for the blocks that are cleaned at common expense, the *amphodarchai* shall take a security and

give the document of the pledge to the *astynomoi* on the same day or on the next. (97) If no one swears that the confiscated goods are his within five days, they shall sell them in the *phratry* or in the full market in the presence of the *astynomoi* and must convey the resulting [...] (102)

Col. III

They shall inspect them (?) and if they find they (?) are in need of repair, the owners shall repair them (?). (105) If any of them refuses, the *astynomoi* with a volunteer among those who have suffered damage shall assign the contract. They (the *astynomoi*) shall collect as soon as possible three-fifths of the ensuing expenses from the person who did not comply, two-fifths from the other and hand it over to the contractors. (112) When common walls are in need of repair or have fallen down, if the neighbors use the walls in the same way, they shall contribute equally to the construction. (116) But if one house abuts the wall, while the other is freestanding, the one whose property leans (against the wall) shall pay two-thirds for the construction, the one whose property is freestanding one-third. (121) Likewise they shall also pay if one has a two-floor-structure, and the other a one-floor-structure. (123) There shall be right of indictment before the *astynomoi* on the issue of common walls against the one who damages them and, if the defendants are found liable, having been defeated in a legal procedure, they shall pay the damage caused to those (structures). (127) No one shall have the power to build on or cut through or in any other way damage common walls, unless they persuade the owners (to grant permission). (132) As to the neighboring walls that damage those who reside there, if the owners who have courtyards on the side of their neighbors want to build *peristaseis*, (136) they shall not be forbidden to build them [the *peristaseis*] with a width of no more than one cubit and covering them with stone copings, after they have built the outer wall of the *peristasis* securely, if there is no bedrock, where the copings will be laid. (142) While covering [them], they shall not make the foundation higher than the rest of courtyard, lest they block the water. (144) The owners of the *peristaseis* are the builders, while the neighbors (own) the ground above them, when they have been covered, granted that they do not use them in any way, from which derive damages to the other's walls. (149) They shall build the entrances of the *peristaseis* from their own houses. If according to the city architect and the *astynomoi* this is not possible, the neighbors shall provide entrance to those who come in for cleaning, likewise if the walls need repair if they collapsed. (156) Concerning those who enter for the purpose of malice, if they catch them, after the *astynomoi* make a judgment, they shall fine them five drachmas. (159) Nobody shall make trenches, plant pithoi, neither plan nor do anything else to someone else's walls or common walls, which would damage the wall. (163) Otherwise, if the owner files charges, the *astynomoi* shall investigate and make a determination, according to what seems fair to them. (166) As for the walls of other persons' houses that are about to fall, when the neighbors sue [...] the damage [...].

Col. IV

(171) they should compel (them) to clean underground conduits. (172) Fountains: the *astynomoi* shall be responsible for the fountains in the city and the suburban area, both that they are clean and that the underground conduits, which bring the water in and out, remain flowing. (176) If any need maintenance, they shall report it to the *strategoi* and to the official in charge of the sacred revenues, so that through them contracts may be made. (180) It shall not be possible for anyone to water animals, wash clothes, vessels, or any other thing at all at public fountains. (184) Anyone who does any of these things, if he is free, shall be dispossessed of the animals, clothes, and vessels, and be fined fifty drachmas (187); if he is a slave and does any of these things with his owner's approval, he shall be likewise dispossessed and flogged with fifty lashes in the pillory. (191) But if he acts without the owner's approval, he shall be deprived of what he has, and after being whipped with a hundred lashes, he should be detained in shackles for ten days and, when released, he shall be let loose with no fewer than fifty lashes. (196) Among the others to any volunteer (prosecutor) shall belong the right of seizure against all those

who commit an illegal act against fountains; he who takes them or brings the seized property to the *astynomoi* shall be apportioned half of the revenue realized from the seizure, and the rest shall be assigned to the maintenance of the Nymph's sanctuary. (203) Cisterns: after recording the cisterns existing in the houses the *astynomoi* in office shall deposit the records before the *strategoi* in the month Pantheios and see to it that the owners make them waterproof and that none of the extant cisterns are filled (with earth). (209) Otherwise after fining those who do any of those things 100 drachmas per cistern, they shall collect (the money) and compel them to clean them out. (212) If any had been filled in beforehand, they [the *astynomoi*] shall report to the owners, so that they are to clean them within eight months. (215) If they do not do so, after collecting the same fine from them, they shall compel these to clean them out. (217) The resulting revenue of the fines shall be handed in each month to the treasurers and shall be used for the cleaning and maintenance of the cisterns and for nothing else. (221) The *astynomoi* shall compel whoever owns cisterns and by not plastering them damages the neighbors (to plaster the cisterns) and fining them. Also, if mandatory fines arise because of these, after collecting the money, the *astynomoi* shall give it to those who were damaged. (227) As for the *astynomoi* who do not deposit the record of the cisterns in the archive or do not act as the law orders, the *nomophylakes* shall collect 100 drachmas from them and assign it to the same funds. (233) Latrines: the *astynomoi* shall take care of both public latrines and the conduits from them and, for those that are not covered (236) [...].

4 Commentary of the Text of the Astynomoi Law

4.1 The Prescript

L. 1: A prescript whose interpretation has triggered a heated debate introduces the four columns of the Astynomoi law. This fragmentary line runs along the whole width of the stone and is engraved with letters almost twice as large as those in the body of the inscription. The lettering indicates that this was inscribed in the 2nd century A. D., but its content suggests that it must not have been part of the original text passed three centuries earlier, as Fraser, alone, suggested in 1956 without finding consensus or echo to his proposal.[24] The author, too, considers this first line a later addition to the original, Hellenistic law, for reasons explained in the following. Even if it appears straightforward to read, two elements have caused interpretative difficulties, namely the understanding of the word ΑΣΤΥΝΟΜΩΝ and the meaning of the expression βασιλικὸς νόμος.

Morphologically, ΑΣΤΥΝΟΜΩΝ could either be a nominative, masculine, singular participle, ἀστυνομῶν, or a genitive, masculine, plural noun, ἀστυνόμων. The first reading is usually preferred, but Legras and Klaffenbach favored the genitive plural.[25] According to Klaffenbach, the genitive was a further qualification of the expression βασιλικὸς νόμος because *es gab ja schließlich mehr* βασιλικοὶ νόμοι[26] and proposed to restore the line as follows: [ὁ δεῖνα τοῦ δεῖνος ὑπὲρ ἀστυνομία]ς ἀστυνόμων τὸν βασιλικὸν νόμον ἐκ τῶν ἰδίων ἀνέθηκεν.[27] But grammatical and syntactical rules discourage this reading. Firstly, it is unusual to find a genitive preceding the noun it refers to and, even if that had been the case, one would expect an article before it. Another strong argument against Klaffenbach's stand emerged in 1969 when M. Wörrle published *AvP* VIII.3 161.[28] This is a sacred law that survives in two fragments that

---

24 FRASER 1956, pp. 138–139 on which see the severe comment by J. and L. ROBERT *BE* 1958, n. 414.

25 See KLAFFENBACH 1954, p. 11; LEGRAS 1907 who provided only a translation of the text; on Klaffenbach's proposal see J. and L. ROBERT *BE* 1955, n. 188.

26 KLAFFENBACH 1954, p. 11.

27 KLAFFENBACH 1954, p. 25.

28 WÖRRLE 1969, pp. 168–190 and the comments by J. and L. ROBERT *BE* 1971, n. 535–555 (n. 555 focuses on Wörrle's section). For the text now LUPU 2005, pp. 61–65.

were found separately in 1965 (A) and in 1930 (B). Wörrle joined them and dated the resulting inscription to the 2nd century A. D. on paleaographical grounds, although its content is believed to be earlier.[29] The similarities between the Astynomoi law and this text go beyond chronology. The subscript of *AvP* VIII.3 161 strongly resembles the Pergamene prescript by recording the dedication of a *hieronomos*, LL. 36–37, thus: [. .K]λώδιος Γλύκων/ [ἱερ]ονομῶν ἀνέθηκεν.[30] Here, [ἱερ]ονομῶν is clearly a participle and this makes LL. 36–37 an almost perfect parallel to the prescript of the Astynomoi law.[31] On this basis, I take it for certain that the interpretation of ἀστυνομῶν as a participle agreeing with the now lost name of the donor is the better one. It is self-evident that the law had been re-engraved thanks to the private initiative of an entering *astynomos;* it is the meaning of this act that has caused a lenghty discussion still continuing today.[32]

The definition of the Astynomoi law as βασιλικὸς νόμος is, to my best knowledge, unique and qualifies the text temporally and institutionally, namely the document is a *prostagma*[33] of an Attalid king, often identified with Eumenes II, who sponsored several interventions in the city in the attempt to increase its functionality and beauty.[34] A *prostagma* as city-regulation[35] for the activity of local officials who were policing a city

---

29 Lupu 2005 on p. 61 hypothesized that the text could be either a later compilation of differently dated prescriptions for those who visited the Asclepeium or "an updated version of a pre-existing document."

30 "Clodios Glykon dedicated it while *hieronomos.*"

31 See also Wörrle 1969, pp. 187–190.

32 See *supra* p. 4 where I outline the debate and opt for the applicability of the text in the 2nd century A. D. Wörrle 1969, p. 188 asks the same question of *AvP* VIII.3.161 concluding that: "so besteht doch eine gewisse Möglichkeit, daß (auch) die Lex Sacra aus dem Asklepieion ... nicht nur als ehrwürdiges Dokument einer wieder interessant gewordenen Vergangenheit zum Schmuck des Heiligtums diente, sondern rechtsgültige Ordnung war, die man vielleicht (wie in Delos die Inschrift Sokolowski *LSCG* 59) zum Ersatz einer beschädigten Stellen des unter Trajan oder Hadrian größer und prächtiger gewordenen Heiligtumes ... neu einmeißeln ließ." And he extends his conclusions to the Astynomoi law.

33 On *prostagma* see Gauthier 1993, esp. pp. 42–45; Aymard 1967 (*REA* 1949, 327), pp. 212–213; Holleaux 1942, pp. 203–211.

34 On this see Kosmetatou 2003, pp. 154–174 who reflects on Eumenes' role in and outside Pergamon see esp. pp. 164–165, but see my introduction for a comment on Eumenes II and the Astynomoi law.

35 The Astynomoi law is the most detailed surviving city regulation. See Martin 1974[2] ch. 3. In 1992, the so-called *stele du port* from Thasos, mid 5th century B. C., was published by Duchêne and has been used as comparison since. This

that was also the royal residence, can easily be understood. In the past, scholarship has suggested that this prescript crowned the law to connect the two 'golden ages' of Pergamon in an ideal manner. These shared the beneficial activity and influence of the two men who authored the real birth and rebirth of the city, namely Eumenes and Hadrian.[36] As plausible as it may sound, this hypothesis does not rest on any solid foundation. Firstly, there is no certainty that the law was passed or re-engraved under either of them. Secondly, the adjective *basilikos* must refer only to the nature, *prostagma*, and the chronology of the text, not to an unlikely connection between 'houses'.

4.2 Column I

The upper left corner of the stele is missing and with it 33 lines.[37] Because of this crippling gap, the task of determining the main topic of the column has proven difficult from the first. Still, a long established *communis opinio* holds with reason that this section deals with streets, probably urban ones, in contrast to the second half of the column, which is concerned with roads κατὰ χώραν.

The surviving text starts *in medias res* with provisions against generic offenders, but even without the broader context, these lines can teach us something about the city's building policy, the most recurrent offenses against public ground, and the fines with which they were punished.

LL. 2–7: The grammatical subject of the first two readable lines is lost, but it must have been a board of magistrates subordinate to the *strategoi*. These appear for the first time in the apodosis of the subsequent conditional clause and return whenever a major initiative must

---

seems to report provisions concerning the cleaning of private and public spaces too, but its condition and uncertain readings demand caution. See Duchêne 2000, pp. 42–46, with bibliography *post* 1992; the text has been discussed extensively after the *editio princeps* and several new restorations have been suggested since.

36 Virgilio 1993, p. 111 supported this theory vigorously. Eumenes' and the Attalid memory survived long after 133 B. C., as the well-known inscriptions for Diodoros Pasparos can show, see Hepding 1907, n. 4 and 8, recently Jones 2000, pp. 1–14, Idem 1974, and also Virgilio 1994. In imperial Pergamon, the Attalids became a symbol of the past, which mainly meant a remembrance of a prosperous time; they were a valuable memory in a moment of crisis such as were the years of the Mithridatic wars and their immediate aftermath.

37 Klaffenbach 1954, p. 4.

be taken, often to remedy other, less prominent officials' mistakes. They are also called upon to impose substantial punishments on offenders – among whom one can count subordinate officials.[38] In Pergamon, numerous other documents record their presence before, after and under the Attalid rule. This chronologically extended activity should long ago have discouraged the view according to which they constituted a board of officials chosen by the king.[39] Only in 2003, H. Müller argued persuasively against it and has conclusively shown that civic *strategoi*, unlike the regional ones, were officials elected by the city assembly.[40] This does not diminish their importance; on the contrary, because of their relevant position within the *polis*, kings must have paid attention to who was invested with this office in Pergamon, even if they did not nominate them directly.[41] At the same time, cities, even if nominally independent, were subject to the surveillance of a royal "controller." In Pergamon and in other *poleis* of the Attalid kingdom this was the duty of the so-called *epi tes poleos*, who appears in the Astynomoi law, L. 69, and for whom evidence is slowly growing.[42]

LL. 7–14: These lines do not provide helpful data to firmly establish the topic here treated, but they allow for the assumption that this section dealt with illegal building activity on public ground. If this is correct, LL. 7–14 preserve the final provisions for the removal of illicit construc-

---

38 The *strategoi* are attested in LL. 5; 16–17; 68–69; 177–179; and 205–206.

39 The dossier that preserves a letter of Eumenes to the People of Pergamon and a decree of the *polis* honoring the king as an answer, WELLES *RC* n. 23, provided the basis for this theory and his commentary on p. 113 is its *manifesto*. This old *communis opinio* was first questioned by MÜLLER 2003, esp. pp. 423–433. For example ALLEN 1983, p. 165–174, and esp. p. 166 n. 25, portrayed Pergamon as a city almost completely controlled by royal appointees, *i. e.* the *strategoi*, so that its administrative independence was in fact only a façade. His views that reflect the *communis opinio* are summarized in IDEM 1983, pp. 176–177. City *strategoi* were key officials in Pergamon, only they were not royal appointees. Testimonies to their duties are *AvP* VIII.1.5 (*OGIS* 265); *AvP* VIII.1.156; *AvP* VIII.1.162; *AvP* VIII.1.167 (*OGIS* 299); *AvP* VIII.1.224 (*OGIS* 323); *AvP* VIII.1.249 (*OGIS* 338); *AvP* VIII.2.251; *AvP* VIII.2.255 through which we learn that they routinely acted as proposers. For an explanation of this role of theirs see MÜLLER 2003, esp. pp. 432–433.

40 MÜLLER 2003, esp. pp. 429–430.

41 Prosopographical data on city-*strategoi* is not available. The position of regional *strategoi* was different, for Pergamon see ALLEN 1983, pp. 87–90, SAVALLI 2001(b), pp. 275–287 for general considerations on this office in the Hellenistic period.

42 On the *epi tes poleos* see *infra* my comment to LL. 67–72.

tions by forceful intervention of the local authorities.[43] This hypothesis rests on parallel data provided by several literary sources that list the duties that *astynomoi* had in other cities or that deal more specifically with the problem of over-building or building on public property within the city. Numerous ancient testimonies suggest that this was a plague for Greek *poleis*, for example in Athens it is said to have immensely slowed down the justice system with the many complaints that derived from it.[44] This would support the hypothesis that this section was devoted to urban streets,[45] in contrast to the last lines of the column, which instead treat those in the *chora*.[46] Be that as it may,[47] all the text says with cer-

---

43 HANSEN 1971², p. 192 already for this interpretation.

44 See *Ath. Pol.* 50, 2; or PL. *Leg.*, 763 C-E where the *astynomoi* are those of the ideal city Magnesia. For the slowing down of the courts see PS. XEN. *Const. Athen.* III. 4. ARIST. *Oecon.* 1347a, among the many anecdotes of the II book, recounts that in Athens, Hippias sold back to the residents their own properties with the excuse that they projected onto public ground and thus belonged to the State. Even if this was an over-interpretation of the regulation against illegal buildings on public grounds, it shows the existence of provisions against it.

45 CORSARO 1990, p. 219 talks of ἀποκαταστάσις as it if were a *terminus technicus* which, if we were to apply to the Astynomoi law, would vouch for the traditional interpretation. The term, however, has a wider range of meanings and is not a decisive proof.
The surviving portion of the first column does not provide further evidence on urban streets. The Pergamon excavation is currently focusing on these mainly in the area on the south-east slope, *i. e.* Eumenes' extension of the town, for which see the yearly reports by PIRSON on *AA* and esp. 2008; 2007; 2006. Important data is emerging with the help of the still ongoing *Gassensondagen,* which consist in the analysis of streets' levels through the digging of shafts. A somewhat older but still reliable overview on urban streets is BOHTZ and ALBERT 1975, pp. 471–529 that focus on the development of the Main Street that was doubled in length under Eumenes II. To be consulted also are WULF 1999, esp. pp. 197–199 and RADT 1999(a), pp. 106–110; 1999(b), pp. 309–312 and 1993, pp. 201–210 publishing the results of the excavation of the living quarter and its street-plan. I must point out that it was then thought that Pergamon's streets followed a regular grid, see also WULF 1994, esp. pp. 135–156 and RADT 2001, pp. 47–49 and 1998, pp. 1–16; today, however, this view is changing, see RAECK 2004 and again PIRSON 2008, pp. 99–100.

46 See HENNIG 1995, pp. 235–282.

47 No objections have ever been made to the *communis opinio*, but I wonder whether other explanations are not also possible. A remote possibility could pertain to special events, such as temporary markets put up *ad hoc* for a religious festivity (or other occasions) could have been disruptive enough. Preparations for those involved building temporary structures that perhaps were not taken down in a timely fashion. For markets held during festivals see CHANDEZON 2000, pp. 70–85 whose analysis takes into account the rich epigraphical material; on temporary structures see the Andania Law *LSCG* 65 on which HARTER-UIBOPUU

tainty is that the *astynomoi* had to assign the restoration work within 10 days, after which they had to hand over the money they had collected to contractors who would then restore the obstructed area. The procedure guiding the farming out of a contract appears several times throughout the text and is expressed with the noun ἔκδοσις in conjunction with the verb ποιέω. An alternative to this is the direct use of ἐκδίδωμι.[48] This has a wide range of meanings, but in this inscription assumes the broader meaning of "making a contract, intervene, assign a contract."[49] The procedure seems to be standard: the officials in charge would auction off a job and the contractor who offered the lowest bid would be assigned it. Throughout the inscription, the *astynomoi* are mostly in charge of assigning the contract. Only once did the *strategoi* replace them because they did not follow the law (L. 16), while another time (LL. 178–180) the entire procedure is off the *astynomoi*'s hands because higher officials are in charge, namely the *strategoi* again and the *epi ton hieron prosodon* probably because of the importance of the object to be restored.

LL. 14–20: The *crux* of L. 17 has caused interpretative problems for which scholarship has found no definite solution yet. The passage records provisions against negligent *astynomoi*, whose tasks had to be taken over by the *strategoi.* Ultimately, these were also responsible for fining their subordinates who would have to pay a sum that the inscription words as follows: τὸ δὲ λοιπὸν διάφορον τῆς ἐκδόσεως.[50] The nature and amount of the fine is the subject of a debate that must be briefly recapitulated,

2002, pp. 135–159. Still useful on markets is the contribution by L. de Ligt and P. W. de Neeve 1988, pp. 391–416, see esp. pp. 411–416; Robert *OMS* VI, 1989, pp. 606–608. Recently, Manganaro 2004, pp. 115–122 has published an inscription that testifies to the assignment of spots in a market.

48 See LL. 8; 16; 18; 53 (restored); 83; 93; 106; 180.

49 This use of ἐκδίδωμι and of the periphrasis ἔκδοσιν ποιεῖν is paralleled; a very pointed example is Thür-Taubner *IPArk.* n. 3, 350 B. C. circa from Tegea on the construction work on the local temple. LL. 6–7 of the text read as follows: εἰ δὲ πόλεμος δια/κωλύσει τι τῶν ἔργων τῶν ἐσδοθέντων . . . · the noun *ekdosis* is used in LL. 15–18 and L. 52. Here I cite 15–18 *exempli gratia*: εἰ δ' ἄ[ν] τις ἐπι/συνίστατοι ταῖς ἐσδόσεσι τῶν ἔργων ἢ λυμαίνη/τοι κατ' εἰ δέ τινα τρόπον φθήρων, ζαμιόντω / οἱ ἐσδοτῆρες . . . on p. 23 this text is translated by the editors of the *corpus* thus: "Wenn sich jemand der Vergabe der Baulose entgegenstellt oder Schaden anrichtet, indem er auf irgendeine Weise Zerstörung bewirkt, sollen die Esdoteres eine Strafe verhängen"; on this inscription see also Thür 1984, pp.471–514.

50 Klaffenbach 1954, pp. 11–12 commented thus: "Die Worte τὸ δὲ λοιπὸν διάφορον τῆς ἐκδόσεως sind schlechterdings unverständlich."

if only to prevent the reappearance of older, discarded solutions. Before 1954, commentators assumed that the *astynomoi* took over the payment of the *hemiolion* recorded in L. 11,[51] which however was part of the offenders' fine. Klaffenbach rejected this theory with the claim that it is illogical to have the offenders' fine reduced because of some official's mistakes. His counter-proposal was to expunge λοιπόν and leave τὸ δὲ διάφορον τῆς ἐκδόσεως to indicate the simple cost of restoration, which the *astynomoi* would have had to pay on top of a fine. His solution avoided also any 'discount' for the offenders because this sentence was not tied to the passage preceding it. In other words, by separating these clauses, the fines previously imposed on the residents remained unaffected. As logical as it may be, Klaffenbach's suggestion is problematic because the Astynomoi law contains noticeably few mistakes: expunging a word is always an extreme solution and, in this case, arbitrary.

In 1955, Oliver proposed emending L. 17 thus: ἔ<λ>λοιπον.[52] This solution did not encounter Klaffenbach's favor since it would have meant a new discount for the offenders, which was not acceptable.[53] Even if I agree with Klaffenbach about Oliver's solution, his 1954 proposal is hardly acceptable as it tampers with an overall correct text.

The only other solution, although this is far from perfect, is to retain the Greek as it is. As it stands, the text could signify that, because the *astynomoi* did not do their job properly – or not at all – the *strategoi* had to take over, but, even after assigning the contract, they could still be short of money (?), *i. e.* τὸ δὲ λοιπὸν διάφορον τῆς ἐκδόσεως. The *astynomoi* would have to pay then this "difference" with a fine on top. This leaves untouched the monetary punishment to the residents/offenders too and they would not benefit from the *astynomoi*'s mistakes.

LL.20–23: these few lines conclude the first section with provisions on the collection of fine money on the part of officials. The initial statement does not raise questions, as it is clear that the *nomophylakes* are in

51 On the *hemiolion* see Sosin 2004, pp. 40–42; briefly on this in Andania Harter-Uibopuu 2002, p. 157, n. 49; and Lecrivain 1895, pp. 302–313.

52 Oliver 1955, p. 88, n. 1.

53 Klaffenbach 1958, pp. 24–25.

charge.[54] The second sentence instead has created some degree of confusion. This is a rather over-succinct phrase indicating that the 'same' procedure applies to 'all other offenders.' The ambiguity is evident. Perhaps it means that, when provisions and fines against *astynomoi* were pending, it was the *nomophylakes'* responsibility to collect the money from the offenders these magistrates failed to fine, as well as from the *astynomoi*.[55]

LL.23–29: this section refers to suburban streets and classifies them according to their width, and, I assume, different functions.[56] The first type of street recorded in the text is the so-called λεωφόρος. Ancient sources testify to those in several occasions to indicate major country roads connecting communities.[57] Such must have been the function of the *leophoroi*

54 In Pergamon *nomophylakes* are not often attested and never appear again after the 2nd century B. C. In this law, they appear twice, LL. 21 and 231, to forcibly collect fine-money from the *astynomoi* who, in both cases, neglected their duties in checking on private property of public concern, for example cisterns. Also, when *nomophylakes* appear so does the statement that the procedure must be 'according to the law' that seems to imply a strictly regulated intervention. See CARDINALI 1906, pp. 270–272; for an assessment of the current knowledge we have on these officials see MÜLLER – WÖRRLE 2002, p. 218, n. 108.

55 Thus also KLAFFENBACH 1954, p. 12. One more note on γεινέσθω, L. 22, is due. Before 1954 this verb was transcribed as γείνεσθωσαν. Despite the difficulties it created, it was never corrected. Klaffenbach's reading from his squeeze noted that this preserves the correct form γεινέσθω, which then must have been simply copied wrongly.

56 HENNIG 2000, pp. 585–587 discusses terminology for Greek streets; also IDEM 1995, 248–253. More recently on the theme LOLOS 2003, pp. 137–154, but esp. pp. 141–142. Occasionally, scholars claim that streets are typical Roman infrastructures, recently LOHMANN 2002, pp. 109–112. This position rests on ancient literary sources, which at times downplay Greek activity in the construction of roads. The Astynomoi law contradicts this view and see the comment by DAVERIO ROCCHI 2002, pp. 148–159, esp. p. 148 on the belittling words of Strabo, STRAB. V 3.8 = 273 C, on Greek roads: "Pertanto, nonostante la difficoltà a disegnare una mappa stradale della Grecia antica e a ricostruire sistematicamente una tipologia funzionale, il giudizio di Strabone deve essere attenuato."

57 λεωφόροι appear often in literary sources, for example PL. *Leg.* 763 C or in several occasions in Pausanias, for example 8.10.01; 8.54.10; 10.35.5 and many others. For an ancient definition see HSCH. *s.v.* λεωφόροι and SUDA *s.v.* λεωφόροι; for a modern one see LOLOS 2003, pp. 141–142; 144 and 156–7; HENNIG 2000, pp. 585–587. Epigraphical instances are instead extremely rare, even if this term was used well into the Roman period and retained the same meaning, for example *SEG* 38, 1244. This is a letter that records an appeal of the citizens of Euippe to Antoninus Pius to take steps against soldiers who did not keep on the highways (*basilikas kai leophorous*), but went into the city, see LOLOS 2003, p. 144.

recorded in the law, as the prescribed width, which is the only detail the document provides, suggests. The text orders that *leophoroi* should not be narrower than 20 πήχεις, which correspond to about 10 meters or thirty feet. The second type of street is called by the generic name of αἱ δὲ ἄλλαι (ὅδοι) and must not be less than 8 πήχεις, *i. e.* 4 meters or twelve feet. Finally, a third group of roads is mentioned. These are small streets (ἀτραπός) for which no minimum width appears.[58] Instead, their function is quickly sketched: they were passageways, in Greek δίοδος, that locals would use to cross over from property to property, which are called γειτνίασις, a term that can mean neighborhood too. Here, however, these were not quarters, but sparsely inhabited parcels of land connected by smaller pathways. The term γειτνίασις appear again later in the text, in L. 32, and refers to the same type of space.[59] This word is rarely attested, yet it has different meanings.[60] In the literary sources, it signifies often neighborhood or can assume an adjectival form and means 'neighbouring.'[61] In inscriptions it is equally rare and can indicate boundaries between cities' territories.[62] Finally, in the Astynomoi law, the significance of 'district, area' is fairly clear in the first case, while in its second appearance, L. 32, seems to have a slightly different meaning. There, it indicates the perimeter of the district defined by the street.[63] In other words, it marks the boundaries of the area that it could be describing, not the area itself.

---

58 A comment by Lolos 2003, pp. 149–151.

59 In Saba 2008, pp. 79–90, esp. pp. 89–90, I hypothesized that the word could have been used also for city neighborhoods too, and thus indicated a bigger unit than that described by *amphoda*. Now, however, I tend to believe that we should not even think in terms of neighborhoods for Pergamon's urban space and living quarters, at least not in the modern sense.

60 See Harland 2003, pp. 22–112.

61 See Plut. *Cor.* 24.

62 See for example *AvP* VIII. I. 245, L. 6 that attempts to regulate the boundaries between Mytilene and Pitane. Another example comes from Priene *I.Pr.* 42, now in Ager 1996, esp. pp. 450–457, n. 160 dated to around 133 B. C. that records the attempt to establish anew the confines between Priene and Samos. For Rhodes' intervention in this long controversy see now Magnetto 2008, with a useful reconstruction of the sequence of the events and the inscriptions testifying to them on p. 71. In *I.Pr.* 42, this term appears at III. LL. 8–9, although partly in restoration, to describe a portion of land within the *chora*.

63 Hennig 1995, p. 249 translates γειτνίασιν as *Straßenfront*.

LL.29–35: state the necessity to maintain streets clean and passable. In the past, scholarship has discussed how this was done and on what scale, but only recently Hennig and Wörrle were able to clarify the second issue by proposing a new restoration for L. 32.

The sentence opens with a verb followed by its object and then by a subject that causes difficulties, LL. 31–32, since not only it is constituted by a few elements, but is also partly corrupted. In 1904, Keil, later followed by Klaffenbach, corrected Kolbe's original reading, in which an ι was restored to reconstruct the expression παρὰ τὰς ο<ἰ>/[κίας]. Keil objected to this and suggested reading the corrupted part as παρὰ τὰς ὁ[δούς] because of the logic of the passage.[64] The restored παρὰ τὰς ὁ[δούς] is part of the grammatical subject, οἱ τὰ κτήματα κεκτημένοι, and provides a location for the properties (τὰ κτήματα) under discussion. The subject reads as follows: "the owners of the land adjoining the streets." This, however, does not solve all reading problems, since we are still left with the puzzling lacuna that contained a number of *stadia* in LL. 32–33. According to Klaffenbach, landowners were not only responsible for the cleaning of the streets around their property, but also farther away for several, unspecified *stadia.* In his *addenda*, Dittenberger justly revealed his skepticism for an interpretation that would pose too heavy a burden on landowners (*nemo credet*), and so did Hennig decades later, saying that Klaffenbach's solution was hard to envision, if only for practical reasons.[65] A solution to the faltering logic of the passage's interpretation has been suggested by Hennig and Wörrle with a new restoration in L. 32. This entails the replacement of the normally accepted conjunction καί, which was always considered too short for the gap, with the preposition κατά. The text would read: "those who own land adjoining the streets shall keep these clean and passable along (κατά) the front of the street for a distance of [.] *stadia* by contributing and working together."[66] The lost number of *stadia* would then refer to the area within which this provision was applicable, not to the area the owners were supposed to clean.

---

64 These were not urban, densely built areas.

65 Hennig 1995, p. 249; Klaffenbach 1954, p. 13.

66 Hennig 1995, pp. 249–250 provides a german translation too.

4.3 Column II

Despite the damages the stone has incurred, the surviving part of this column still preserves important details such as the solutions that the authorities envisioned to ease some of the daily problems afflicting the city that increased the difficulties of a proper maintenance. I must also draw attention to the first readable lines where a remarkable institutional feature appears, namely the magistrates called *amphodarchai,* who are otherwise rarely attested. More precisely, these are almost unique since, outside Roman Egypt, they appear only in Pergamon. According to the law, they were in charge of the surveillance of basic territorial units, *amphoda*, whose careless residents caused damage with self-serving acts to which the provisions of this column tried to put an end.[67]

LL.48–65: The missing upper, left corner of the stone deprives us of the first 15 lines of the text after which additional provisions on cleaning appear, just as at the end of the first column. The focus, however, shifts from the care of suburban streets to the responsibilities of magistrates within city limits.

The first five lines are heavily restored and may already record the curious office of *amphodarchia*, which returns out of lacuna in L. 53 and has attracted scholarly attention. In Pergamon, the *amphodarchai* were local magistrates in charge of *amphoda,* which were not streets, as has been held in the past, but blocks.[68] The term *amphodon* appears only once in the Astynomoi law, col. II L. 92, while its magistrates, the *amphodarchai*, appear three times, LL. 49; 53; 76 and absolve different tasks, which I find useful here to review. In LL. 53–54, an *amphodarches* helps the *astynomoi* to assign a contract, on the nature of which we are not otherwise informed, and to collect fines from residents who had littered

[67] For this magistracy and territorial units see SABA 2008. A *corrigendum* is necessary: on p. 82 *I.Beroia* 41 is wrongly dated to the 2nd century B. C. instead of to the 2nd century A. D. The conclusions reached in the article do not change, but with the right date, the inscription shows another important side as it testifies to the existence of these territorial units in Beroia up to the 2nd century A. D. just as the Astynomoi law does for Pergamon.

[68] On *amphoda* see SABA 2008, pp. 79–90 for the epigraphical data, DU BOUCHET 2004, pp. 43–55 on philological evidence. More on *amphoda infra* in my comment on L. 92.

and then refused to clean up.[69] In this passage, we learn that the *amphodarchai* acted alone, or, in other words, each *amphodarches* was in charge of an *amphodon*. These magistrates appear again in L. 75 and are the subject of the apodosis of a conditional clause whose protasis is of difficult interpretation. The clause deals with damages that residents caused to the street paving, for example by leaving conduits uncovered. It was the *amphodarchai's* responsibility to stop them from such acts. Finally, in L. 94 they initiated the repossession of the goods of residents who did not contribute the due amount for the cleaning of *amphoda* or did not pay the fines tied to this. Also, they were eventually responsible for selling these goods under the supervision of the *astynomoi*. A few considerations are needed here. *Amphodarchai* appear twice in the plural, busy with duties that they all had, but surely could discharge individually. Moreover, in the last instance, the plural follows the only reference to *amphoda* and must have been a generic indication (L. 92). This leads me to assume that the *amphodarchai* did not work as a board in Pergamon, but each of them took care of a block and was subordinate to the authority of the *astynomoi*, whose higher rank is shown by the fact that they could fine any negligent *amphodarches*. For example, in LL. 56–59, the *astynomoi* fine them 20 *drachmae* for each misdeed they may have committed. The resulting money was handed over to the treasurers monthly and could be spent for the cleaning of the streets (?) only.[70] This last detail is only warranted by a commonly accepted restoration of LL. 63–64: εἰς τὴν ἀνακάθαρσ[ι]ν / [τῶν οδῶν . . .], although it would be worthwhile considering also Klaffenbach's restoration τῶν τόπων.[71] This is a viable hypothesis, since in Greek ἀνακάθαρσις could be used to indicate the cleaning of very different structures.[72] For example, in Mylasa it refers

[69] In L. 54 I follow Klaffenbach's restoration [τὸ γενόμενον ἀνάλωμα] instead of the formerly accepted [τὸ διάφορον ἡμιόλιον]. This should have been introduced with καὶ ἐκτός in analogy with L. 19. The text asserts that the *amphodarchai* had to force those who littered to clean up. The object of the littering has been differently restored, L. 49 on which see also KLAFFENBACH 1954, p. 13, in this regard I am inclined to agree with this scholar's preference for the more general noun κόπρος.

[70] For a similar provision see *infra* col. IV LL. 219–221, and SABA, 2008, p. 88. In L. 60 the money coming from the fines is worded as follows: [δὲ γεινόμενα δ]ιάφορα, which KLAFFENBACH 1954, p. 13 thought too short. Yet, he also added "die Buchstabenabstände schwanken in der Tat in dieser Inschrift."

[71] See KLAFFENBACH 1954, p. 13.

[72] See HELLMANN 1992(a), pp. 45–46 on this term in and outside Delos.

to the cleaning of a well, ἀνακάθαρσις τοῦ φρέα/[του],[73] in an inscription from Didyma an ἀνακάθαρσις λατομίου is attested or in Ephesos we hear of an ἀνακάθαρσις τοῦ λιμένου.[74] In the Astynomoi law, the restoration [τῶν οδῶν . .] relies exclusively on its proximity to the end of column I where streets were the main topic. The focus of column II, however, has shifted to other themes. I cannot be certain that τῶν τόπων is the correct solution, but it is supported by line 50 where the *amphodarchai* had to ἀνακαθαίρειν τὸν τ]όπον.[75]

LL.65–66: These lines establish additional duties with which the *astynomoi* had to engage if the *amphodarchai* failed. Two elements are noteworthy here: firstly, the *astynomoi* have the responsibility to exact all the monies coming from fines, which is a parallel to LL. 20–21, and shows that they had a key role in local administration. The second note pertains to the genitive τῶν ἄλλων / [πάντ]ων of LL. 65–66 that refers to additional tasks for the *astynomoi* and needs a comment. This is a very generic, and puzzling, reference that could mean that the *astynomoi* were in charge of the *amphoda* and their cleanliness *pro tempore*, if the *amphodarchai* failed to attend to their duties. A transfer of responsibilities is not unparalelled in the law, since this establishes that negligent *astynomoi* may see their duties temporarily assigned to *strategoi*. It is, however, the first instance of delegation of authority to the *astynomoi*. Possibly, this was a standard procedure at all levels: if magistrates failed to attend to their duties, their direct superiors had to intervene and take them over.

LL.67–72: conclude the first part (?) of the column by listing additional, but common provisions against careless magistrates. Earlier in the text, the *astynomoi* were said to be in charge of punishing negligent *amphodarchai* and, possibly, taking care of their duties *pro tempore*.

73 Blümel 2004, p. 5, the text dates to the 3rd B. C.

74 *I.Didyma* 40+41, LL. 16–17 according to the editor, the lettering allows saying that this is *gute hellenistische Schrift*; *I.Ephesos* 3071, LL. 11–12 mid of the III century A. D.

75 In the past, scholarship has compared the *amphodarchai* with the Athenian *hodopoioi*. According to the *Ath. Pol.* 54, these were five magistrates drawn by lot whose main duty was the care of streets with the help of public slaves. Although the *amphodarchai* were also responsible for streets, their duties were broader and are anyway set in a different institutional context. See also Saba 2008, p. 88.

Here, however, the law goes further and states that if the *astynomoi* failed as well, they would be subject to punishment. Of particular interest is the official who, together with the *strategoi*, is in charge of fining them, namely ὁ ἐπὶ τῆς πόλεως.

The *strategoi* are well-known in and outside Pergamon as high-ranking officials who could act, with different duties, at a regional level as royal appointees, or at a *polis* level. In this case, they were city magistrates and the general assembly elected them.[76] The position and function of the ἐπὶ τῆς πόλεως is less clear. The evidence has only recently started to grow and Müller and Wörrle have offered a first analysis of it.[77] The occasion for their scrutiny was the publication of a new epigraphic document that dates between 168/6–166/4 B. C. and contains fragmentary provisions tied to sacrifices and events of a religious association within Pergamene possessions.[78] The first surviving lines record the award of crowns to the royal couple and following hierarchic order list other honorees who were sacred and secular officials.[79] Among them also figures the ἐπὶ τῆς πόλεως. This is only the last of several inscriptions that have come to light in the past 15 years to attest to the presence of this magistrate in the Attalid Kingdom.[80] Testimonies have been found scattered throughout its possessions, from remote locations such as the city of Olbasa in Milyas to practically central areas, such as Caria where Tralles had an *epi tes poleos*.[81] To these texts, we should add the long-known document from

76 See supra my comment on LL. 2–7.

77 See Müller-Wörrle 2002, pp. 223–227.

78 Müller-Wörrle 2002, p. 194.

79 LL. 7–12: [σ]τέφανοι δὲ ἀνακηρυσσέσθωσαν μετὰ τὸ δεῖπνο̣[ν τῆι – ca 6 –] / [ἡ]μέραι ὑπὸ τῶν ἀρχεπιμηνίων βασιλεῖ Ἀττάλωι κα[ὶ βασιλίσ]/σηι Ἀπολλωνίδι θεοῖς· βασιλεῖ, βασιλίσσηι, βασιλέως ἀ̣δελ[φοῖς· ἀρ]/χιερεῖ, ἱερεῖ τῆς συνόδου. ἡμιολίῳ̣ι, τῷ̣ι ἐπὶ τῆς πόλεως, διοικηπ[τῆι],/ ἀρχεγλογιστῆι, οἰκονόμωι, ἐγλογισ̣τῆι, ἱερονόμωι, ἀγῳ̣νοθ̣έ̣/τηι, γραμματεῖ. (. . .)

80 See Savalli-Lestrade 2001(a) on the evidence pp. 80–90.

81 The *editio princeps* of the Olbasa's text that dates to the reign of Attalos II is by Kearsley 1994, pp. 47–57. The inscription records a decree honoring Sotas son of Patroklos (LL. 1–22), who was *epi tes poleos* in Olbasa L. 27, and a letter by Attalos (II) giving his approval for this – and another – grant passed by the city (LL. 23–30). Malay 1996, pp. 83–86 published an inscribed ostothek from Tralles that dates to a year after the treaty of Apameia. On it appear two different inscriptions recording the names of the deceased, namely that of Dionysios son of Dionysios, grandson of Theophilos στρατηγὸς τοῦ ὑπαίθρου καὶ ἐπὶ τῆς πόλεως and his wife Hegeanassa daughter of Pyrros, on whom see Müller-Wörrle 2002, pp. 223–224, n. 142. In a second column appear the names of

Aegina that honors Kleon, the *epistates* of the city, and asks for a renewal of his term because of his good services.[82] Kleon must have been the governor of the island, but the peculiar status of Aegina after 202 B. C.[83] calls for caution in using this text as a term of comparison for the office of the ἐπὶ τῆς πόλεως in other areas. In an attempt to establish the role of this official, we could also consider the evidence coming from outside the Attalid reign, such as that from Macedon and the Seleucid realm where *epistatai* τῆς πόλεως are well attested too and may have had similar duties.[84] This evidence informs the current view for which also in Pergamon the ἐπὶ τῆς πόλεως was a royal appointee, or in other words he was the connecting element between the king and the civic administration. His specific role is still difficult to determine,[85] and it is not known whether only a few or all 'dependent', Attalid cities had this magistrate or, if they did not, under what circumstances one was sent there. If the text from Aegina testifies to his presence, one could infer that his duties could impact city life, here positively, with direct interventions.

Dionysios' father, namely Dionysios son of Theophilos, στρατηγὸς Καρίας καὶ Λυδίας τῶν κατὰ Ἔφεσον τόπων, his wife Melitine daughter of Gaudotos and finally the names of another couple whose relation to the former is unclear. These are Athenomoiros son of Demarchos, ἐπὶ τῆς πόλεως, and his wife Tatis daughter of Mithridates, on whom MÜLLER-WÖRRLE 2002, p. 224, n. 144 referring to SAVALLI-LESTRADE 2001(a), pp. 81–88.

82 *OGIS* 329 + GAUTHIER 1993, pp. 41–48, see SAVALLI-LESTRADE 1998, n. 12 on Kleon.

83 SeeALLEN 1971, pp. 1–12.

84 For the Seleucid reign see CAPDETREY 2007, esp. pp. 301–306; also MÜLLER-WÖRRLE 2002, pp. 223–227; for Macedon ERRINGTON 2002, pp. 51–63. In Egypt governors called ἐπὶ τῆς πόλεως are attested, see BAGNALL 1976, p. 222, but seem to have had military duties that we do not find for the Attalid officials by the same name. Studies on Hellenistic reigns tend to focus on individual kingdoms, but a comprehensive assessment of the evidence seems to point to the existence of a common administrative framework that relied on several officials with similar duties and titles.

85 CAPDETREY 2007, p. 306 comments on the evidence from Olbasa as follows: "ce document suggère que le ὁ ἐπὶ τῆς πόλεως attalide exerçait des compétences militaires sur un territoire qui dépassait le cadre urbaine." Capdetrey's statement seems to rest on a reading that conflates the titles of στρατηγὸς τοῦ ὑπαίθρου καὶ ἐπὶ τῆς πόλεως that the inscription records for the deceased. Yet the duties of these offices were different and the deceased must have held them at separate times.

In the Astynomoi law, this magistrate appears only once and acts together with the *strategoi* to decide how heavily irresponsible *astynomoi* had to be fined. Whether one of their duties was to supervise the activity of other civic officials cannot be stated with certainty, but it is an educated guess. Certainly, their involvement in this specific case suggests that, whatever the issue at stake, it must have concerned not only streets, rather the decision must have pertained to a general evaluation of the *astynomoi*'s performance or a matter of greater relevance for the city. This, in turn, reinforces the idea that line 64 should not be restored with the genitive for streets, and possibly not even the restoration τῶν τόπων would be appropriate since it is too generic. The object worthy of the attention of top officials cannot be recovered with certainty, but it could have been of (strategic?) relevance to the city.

L. 72: In this line we find the first of a series of genitives that the law uses to mark new sections.[86] Here the genitive χοός is a secondary form of χοῦς that I translate as 'rubble.'

LL.72–76: The new paragraph lists several illegal activities that residents perpetrated thus damaging public property. It was the *amphodarchai*'s duty to prevent this from happening. The damages that residents inflicted to the infrastructures must have been serious given that they are said to despoil streets by taking away filling material, stones, by making mortar or even taking bricks away.[87] A parallel to this can be found in a passage of the ἀστυνομικὸς μονόβιβλος,*Dig.* 43.10.2, a remarkable text of the period of the Severii that is concerned with the duties of *astynomoi*.[88] Among those (they) ἐπιμελείσθωσαν δὲ ὅπως μηδεὶς ὀρύσσῃ τὰς ὁδοὺς μηδὲ χωννύῃ μηδὲ κτίσῃ εἰς τὰς ὁδοὺς μηδέν. This clause synthesizes several points that the Astynomoi law treats too and reveals that

86 The practice of introducing new sections with representative words or with a periphrasis is not unusual, for example see the Andania law (*LSCG* 65), Deshours 2006, esp. pp. 61–62.

87 Commentators have debated on which verb goes with the accusative λίθους in L. 73 because it seems suspended between ὀρύσσωσιν and ποιῶσιν. Klaffenbach 1954, p. 13 reads λίθους with ὀρύσσωσιν to signify that residents should not take away the stones used to pave streets. This hypothesis seems plausible. Also, the paragraph insists on the problem of 'open conduits', on which see *infra* LL. 90–93. On the terminology see Hellmann 1992 (a), p. 262.

88 Full text and comment in the appendix.

the problems this law tackled in the 2nd century B. C. (and renewed in its purpose three centuries later) were still prevailing under the Severii. The residents' habit of making private use of stolen public material must have been a plague for ancient cities, which desperately tried to defend the integrity of their infrastructures.

LL.76–86: this paragraph contains routine provisions. If residents commited any of the listed offenses, the *amphodarchai* had to report them to the *astynomoi*, who were in charge of fining and forcing them to restore the damaged property to its original condition.

Here I must devote particular attention to a problem that clearly was of great concern to the authorities, namely open conduits. In LL. 80–82, the document states specifically that "offenders had to seal conduits," while any other repair to different damages goes under the generic τά τε ἄλλα ἀποκαθιστάναι εἰς τὰ ἐξ ἀρχῆς. Moreover, these lines establish a heavier punishment and higher fine, ἡμιόλιον, for those who persisted in their negligent behavior. Finally, it must be noted that the *astynomoi* were again in charge of assigning the contract for the restoration of the damaged structures within ten days.

LL. 86–88: these lines dwell on one of the *amphodarchai*'s duties that was already listed in LL. 72–76, namely surveilling the integrity of conduits (*ochetoi*).

In LL. 74–75, the law prescribes that the *amphodarchai* stop residents from making μετεώρους ὀχετούς. Additionally, they had to ensure that these would make the conduits already in place κρυπτούς, which I rendered as 'underground'. In brief, if 'open' conduits were there, residents had to 'close' them.[89] In Greek, *ochetoi* are both conduits and drains,[90] but this section of the Astynomoi law must refer to drains coming out of houses that were built illegally and remaining on the streets, *i. e.* public ground. More problematic on the other hand is the attempt to establish the meaning of the two adjectives, μετέωρος and κρυπτός that qualify *ochetoi*. In the past, Kolbe misunderstood their significance, probably reinforced by an earlier inaccurate interpretation of a passage from the *Ath. Pol.* 50.2. prescribing that the Athenian *astynomoi* hinder, among

89 Briefly on this again Hennig 1995, p. 253.
90 A detailed overview is in Argoud, 1983, pp. 7–9.

other things, residents from building open conduits that go on to the street (ὀχετοὺς μετεώρους εἰς τὴν ὁδὸν ἔκρουν ἔχοντας ποιεῖν.) Kolbe must have followed an older, inaccurate translation and read the adjective (plus noun) as if it meant: "Wasserrinnen in der Höhe"; later, however, Klaffenbach and Martin rectified this mistake.[91]

More recently, Argoud has helped to clarify their significance with an analysis of *IG* VII 4255. This is a text from Oropos concerned with structural improvements to the sanctuary.[92] Of interest are LL. 4–5 that order the construction of a ὀχετὸμ ποῆσαι λίθινον κ/ρυπτόν that should have allowed discharging water from a bath. Through the study of numerous examples, Argoud concludes that the two adjectives (μετεώρους, κρουπτούς) *do not* describe different types of *ochetoi*, but only their position in relation to the ground. In other words, an *ochetos kryptos* is buried underground, while a *meteoros* rests on the surface.[93] The latter were not allowed in Pergamon or, more precisely, the authorities tried to stop residents from building them on public ground. In L. 86 then the participle προϋπάρχοντας suggests that the provision was intended to be retroactive. The authorities wanted to eliminate all *ochetoi* lying on public ground, most likely because they might impede traffic (?).[94] These surface drains must have been very common and constituted a real problem to prompt such forceful provisions against them.

So far the text: in 1957, Martin also used findings from the excavations in Priene, Delos and Olynthos to corroborate his philological work on the two adjectives. Although Argoud's work is illuminating, Martin's methodology must be applied to the case of Pergamon and provide an overview of the results of the archaeological research in Pergamon to see whether we can find a confirmation on the ground of this reading of the two adjectives and the text. Luckily, the articulated water distribution

---

91 See MARTIN 1974^2, pp. 66–81, esp. pp. 66–72; KLAFFENBACH 1954, p. 13.

92 Now in PETRAKOS 1997, n. 292. The text dates to a year between 335 and 322 B. C.

93 ARGOUD 1983, p. 8: "c'est plutôt une indication de situation qui est ainsi soulignée: la conduite n'est plus enterrée, mais placée sur le sol, en surface." So also HELLMANN 1999, n. 2.

94 On this see *D.* 43.10 in the app. *infra*.

system of Pergamon has been studied in detail and its results published in full.[95]

Many of the water conduits that ran in and through the city were located underneath streets as the *Gassensondagen* have shown, *i. e.* the archeological mission in Pergamon has been digging shafts in the streets that have revealed the presence of different types of water conduits located under the paving.[96] This is still work in progress, but partial results have been published in the meantime. *Gassensondagen* have been undertaken in the Main Street[97] underneath which a major conduit allowed for the collection and flow of water coming from the adjoning structures and inhabited areas. The water was not channeled directly from each building into the main conduit, but to several minor conduits that run parallel to it to converge later. These are all sealed, cylindrical conduits with different diameters and capacity. Also, they are all located underneath the street and covered with thick slabs of stone.[98]

The main conduit must have been a ὑπόνομος. *Hyponomoi* appear also in the law at beginning of the IV column[99] and indicate channels dug underground meant to transport larger quantities of water. The law says for example that they serviced fountains and latrines. The difference between *ochetoi* and *hyponomoi* is well explained by Knoepfler in his commentary on the famous Chaerephanes inscription from Eretria that dates to a year between the end of the 4th and the beginning of the 3rd century B. C.[100] In regard to conduits, Knoepfler writes: "*ochetos* désigne normalement une canalisation (quel que soit le matériau utilisé) et non pas un canal creusé."[101] Knoepfler then supports the idea of a structural difference between *ochetoi* and *hyponomoi*. One can go a step further and add to his observations that while *ochetoi* could rest on the surface,

---

95 The volume *AvP* 1, 2 published by GARBRECHT in 2001 provides a detailed analysis of Pergamon's water system and the different infrastructures that had been built already under the Attalids to bring water to the hill. In the final bibliography I recorded several of his earlier contributions on specific aspects of this city's water system that must be consulted.

96 See RADT 1996, p. 444 for a definition of *Gassensondage*.

97 See just as an example BOHTZ and ALBERT 1975, pp. 472–502.

98 See BOHTZ and ALBERT 1975 for the major streets, RADT 1996, esp. p. 444.

99 LL. 171; 175; and 235.

100 On this text see the commentary by KNOEPFLER 2001, pp. 41–80.

101 KNOEPFLER 2001, p. 53 where he discusses possible restorations for L. 22 of this text.

hyponomoi could not and that in general they must have had a greater capacity than the *ochetoi*. These, for example, could describe also the pipes and channels that brought pluvial water down to cisterns.[102]

LL.88–90: the last two lines of the paragraph contain the usual provisions against negligent *astynomoi*. In this case, the text does not specify who was in charge of fining them, but by default one must assume it was the *strategoi*. Klaffenbach has already noted that the wording indicates that the *astynomoi* were not to be fined a higher sum than the offenders (αὐτοὶ -*astynomoi*- ἔνοχοι ἔστωσαν ταῖς ἴσαις ζημίαις), which is peculiar, since normally fines against officials were higher than those against residents.[103]

L.90: the genitive πράξεως opens a new section. The term has a wide range of meanings,[104] but here "collection" as in forcible collection is possibly the best rendering of this title; another translation could be instead "recovery of money." This section must have continued to the end of the column, which, however, is not completely preserved.[105]

LL.90–93: the apodosis of a long conditional clause follows the genitive πράξεως and sets the tone of the subsequent provisions. The new paragraph concerns the legal consequences that the residents who did not 'give their accrued share of the contract (for the collection) of dung or of the fines for the streets/neighborhood cleaned at common expense' had to face. The repercussions were serious, since offenders could be liable to the seizing of their goods (*enechyrasia*).[106] Public cleaning emerges repeatedly in the first two columns, which suggests that this was a concern to the authorities. The reiterated provisions and threats of penalties were

---

102 For a definition of *hyponomos* see ORLANDOS and TRAVLOS 1986, p. 259. Useful is CHATELAIN's 2001, esp. pp. 83–89, discussion of this term's meaning in the ancient literary, epigraphical and papyrological sources and also WÖRRLE 1981, pp. 83–84 commenting a group of Attic *horoi* already studied by KLAFFENBACH 1961, pp. 121–126 on the rights to water's use. ORLANDOS and TRAVLOS 1986, p. 196 provide a definition of *ochetos*.

103 KLAFFENBACH 1954, p. 14.

104 See BRAVO 1980, pp. 702–704.

105 Se also SABA 2011, esp. pp. 12–21.

106 On the two possible meanings of *enechyrasia* as seizing of goods and security as a pledge see again BRAVO 1980, p. 703 and HARRISON 1971, esp. pp. 244–247 whose focus is Athens.

clearly considered a necessary tool to force residents to attend to their duties. At the same time, the text conveys the impression that this *polis* expected a strong commitment on part of residents to keep its spaces clean.[107]

LL. 90–93 are not in fact devoted to cleaning, but to the procedure regulating the forcible collection of money or seizing of goods, if residents did not abide by the law, nevertheless a few details on public cleaning can be extrapolated. One important point concerns the fact that residents had to contribute, possibly financially, to the cleaning of territorial units (*amphoda*) as this was done 'κοινῇ', LL. 90 93.[108] Incidentally, this is the only citation of *amphoda* in the text. These territorial units are not of easy definition and scholars have identified them alternatively with streets or blocks. I have already argued in print that the last interpretation is to be preferred also in light of the original meaning of the word as "streets of houses," which implies more than a street by including terrain lots.[109] *Amphoda* are attested in several Greek cities in the Hellenistic time and later too. For example, texts from Stratonikeia and Smyrnae that date to the 3rd and 2nd century B. C. record them and mark their territorial limits.[110] In the case of Smyrnae these units helped to define the extension of military areas. More revealing of their physical extension is the decree *IGLS* IV, 1261 from Laodikeia by the Sea in Syria where an *amphodon* is said to be big enough to contain a *temenos*.[111] This suggests that it was more than a street and certainly not linear in extention.

To return to cleaning, the loss of the upper half of the first column of the law has probably deprived us of the regulation on the maintenance of urban streets. It is possible that its organization was not very different from that of the streets κατὰ χώραν attested in the first column LL. 29–35, at least in principle. If that was the case, it is reasonable

[107] Indications on how to keep streets in the *chora* clean appear in column one, LL. 29–30, and throughout column two, LL. 48–72.

[108] On *amphoda* see SABA 2011, pp. 215 and 217; EADEM 2008, pp. 87–90; DU BOUCHET 2004, pp. 43–55. For the *amphodarchai* see the commentary to LL. 48–65.

[109] DU BOUCHET 2004, pp. 43–55 for a complete philological analysis.

[110] *I. Strat.* 1004 3rd–2nd century B. C.; *I. Smyrna* II.1 613; 613b; 613c 3rd–2nd century B. C.

[111] *IGLS* IV, 1261 175 B. C., see SOSIN 2005, pp. 130–139.

to assume that in Pergamon residents were expected to contribute substantially to the cleaning of public spaces, *amphoda* or streets, be that as manpower or financially.[112] In the recent past, Hennig has reached this same conclusion and asserted that authorities used both residents' manpower and money to keep the city clean. It can indeed be assumed that the city used the money collected from the fines listed in LL. 59–65 and 70–72 of this column to finance the cleaning of spaces for which locals could not be held directly responsible.[113] Otherwise, residents had to keep their property clean. In other words, the city of Pergamon relied on the active involvement of its residents.

Sources on public cleaning throughout the Greek world are scarce; evidence comes from very few places, among which Athens stands out.[114] How it worked is unknown, but the *Ath. Pol.* mentions officials and their subordinates or helpers in charge. In the section devoted to the Athenian *astynomoi,* the text says (§ 50): (the *astynomoi* σκοποῦσιν) ὅπως τῶν κοπρολόγων μηδεὶς ἐντὸς ι′ σταδίων τοῦ τείχους καταβαλεῖ κόπρον

[112] The Stele of the Harbor of archaic Thasos appears to treat similar issues. According to DUCHÊNE's 1992 uncertain restoration, the responsibility for cleaning was shared between the legal owner of a property and the [*epistatai*] who helped once a month. We can hardly treat this text as a parallel, however, both because of its chronology (5th century B. C.) and because it is too fragmentary. See LEWIS 1993, pp. 402–403 and HENNIG 1995, p. 237 esp. n. 237, and again on pp. 237–242 and, finally, DUCHENE 2000, pp. 42–46.
Two other inscriptions from Thasos must be mentioned, namely *IG* XII.8.265 and *IG* XII Suppl. p. 152 (*LSCG* 115). VATIN 1976, p. 559 has discussed their chronology in detail, but here it suffices to say that the first must be older than the second, which dates to the beginning of the 3rd century B. C. They record rent agreements for an area described as the 'Gardens of Herakles' and intend to rectify pre-existing accords by specifying that the tenant had to keep clean an area by a gate where, apparently, normally rubbish was deposited, LL. 3–4. The second inscription must refer to the same area, but this must have been enlarged with the addition of another plot that the tenant was also supposed to keep clean. This second text, however, is rather fragmentary, which makes it hard to understand exactly other possible responsibilities of the tenant and their regulation. VATIN 1976, p. 563 hypothesized that the tenant either saw his rent reduced for his services or did not pay at all; for HENNIG 1995, p. 242, n. 24 this is *sehr hypotetisch.* Finally, in both inscriptions officials are in charge to check that the tenant actually performed his duties.
On Herakles' cult in Thasos see JOURDAIN-ANNEQUIN 1998, pp. 351–355, on the sanctuary in particular see BERGQUIST's 1973 work.

[113] HENNIG 1995, pp. 250–252, see esp. n. 54 with further references and examples.

[114] See LIEBESCHUETZ 2000, pp. 54–57; LINDENLAUF 2000; HENNIG 1995, pp. 246–248;VATIN 1976, pp. 555–558.

ἐπιμελοῦνται. Athens used the service of these *koprologoi*, scavengers (?), to take the collected garbage outside the city walls to a distance of minimum 2 Km. Probably, dumps or dumping grounds were located there. The institutional role of the *koprologoi* is unknown, but I exclude the idea that they were members of an office as it was hypothesized in the past on the basis of a Demosthenic passage.[115] Instead, it is more logical to assume that they were private individuals who were either paid by the city to discharge this duty or that they maybe sold the garbage thus collected as fertilizer (?).

The *Ath. Pol.* 50 also lists other duties of the Athenian *astynomoi* that pertain to street maintenance,[116] but were not directly related to cleaning. Athens had indeed other officials called *hodopoioi* whose responsibilities we find listed in *Ath. Pol.* (§ 54): κληροῦσι δὲ καὶ τάσδε τὰς ἀρχάς· ὁδοποιοὺς πέντε, οἷς προστέτακται δημοσίους ἐργάτας ἔχουσι τὰς ὁδοὺς ἐπισκευάζειν. There were five of them in charge of the streets and they used the help of public slaves. In Athens the two offices of *astynomia* and *hodopoia* must have shared the responsibility of street maintenance and for manual tasks public slaves were employed.[117] Private owners on the other hand must have been responsible for the upkeep of their properties and the areas immediately adjoining them, but direct evidence is lacking. In other words, the sources convey the impression that Athenian public cleaning relied less on residents and more on an organized public system. It must be said, however, that since this city was patently bigger than Pergamon, probably it was hard to control the territory and the activity of its residents as efficiently.

---

115 Hennig 1995, p. 247 with several hypotheses on their actual status, on which already Vatin 1976 p. 558. For the remote possibility that they were officials see [Demosth.], *Contra Arist.* XXV, 49.

116 See *infra* the section on the Athenian *astynomia*.

117 Inscriptions testify to this duty for *astynomoi*. *IG* II^2 380, LL. 34–39 forbade that people throw rubbish or perpretate another act difficult to define, LL 37–38, in the agora and the *astynomoi* had to see to it that they did not. On possible readings for these lines see Vatin 1976, p. 557, according to whom "En réalité, le réglement ne concerne pas l'installation ou l'entretien de depots d'ordures, mais l'interdiction de souillier le voie publique: [μήτε] κοπρῶ/[σαι μήτ' ἐ]ν τῆι ἀγορᾶι [μήτ'ἐν τα]ῖ[ς ὁ]δοῖς." This and other texts, *IG* II^2 659 and 704, assert that the *astynomoi* had to supervise religious processions and, one can assume, their route. It is possible that in Athens the *astynomoi* dealt with streets only under special circumstances.

As it is, there is not enough evidence to create a "model" for a possible public cleaning system in the ancient world, but I can still point out the different patterns that have emerged. Pergamon seems to have relied on a direct contribution of its residents. So must Athens, but only partially, since the city had a more structured system at the administrative level with the presence of officials and personnel in charge of performing the actual cleaning. The city-size must have been a decisive factor in the way the system was organized, but overall one can detect a mixture of public and private responsibility.

LL.94–101: syntactically these lines are the apodosis of the conditional clause that describes the procedure for the seizing of the goods belonging to residents who acted unlawfully. The *amphodarchai* initiated the procedure by taking a pledge and had to hand over a document of repossession to the *astynomoi* within two days. These had to make the repossession known to the public and, if nobody claimed the goods back within five days, the *amphodarchai* had to sell them in an auction that took place in the phratry or in the "full market."[118]

L. 97 uses the verb ἐξόμνυμι that could signify "to swear in excuse" or is attested also as *terminus technicus* in legal discourse for "deny, abjure."[119] In the Astynomoi law, the verb entails the presence of a third party who swears that the confiscation was illegal because the

118 See KLAFFENBACH 1954, p. 14; HITZIG 1905, pp. 437–441. On *enechyrasia* see BRAVO 1980, pp. 693–704. Also, see *P. Hal.* 1 LL. 234–241 on which *infra*. GARCIA MORCILLO 2005, pp. 21–39 provides a brief overview of the evidence on sales through auctions in the Greek world, esp. pp. 24–25. She cites the Astynomoi law as if it attested to a standard procedure; yet what we know from Pergamon is rather generic and using it as main reference only shows how little we know. See also SABA 2011, pp. 19–21.

119 In the Greek world *exomosia* entailed an oath with a "disclaimer." For example, in Delphi magistrates who wanted to be excused from sentencing swore this oath, see SALVIAT – VATIN 1971, pp. 58–60. The procedure appears in several areas of the Greek world and is well attested in Athens too, for which see MARTIN 2008, pp. 56–68; RUBINSTEIN 2005, pp. 107–110, with THÜR's comments in the same volume, esp. pp. 122–123, CARY 1995, pp. 114–119. ARMONI 2005, p. 214 discusses a papyrus of uncertain provenance, *PSI Com.* VI 11 dated to 185–180 B. C., and recognizes a case of *exomosia* similar to that attested in the Astynomoi Law and in *P. Eleph.* 23 (222 B. C.). *P. Eleph.* 23 records the complaints of a Paniskos whose land was taken away by the authorities because they thought it belonged to another man named Psentaeas. Paniskos swore, however, that it was his own. CASA 2008, esp. p. 427, n. 2 and pp. 453–454 disagrees with Armoni's interpretation of *PSI Com.* VI 11 and ties the procedure to a well attested Egyptian

property repossessed was not the offender's, but his own.[120] A procedural epigraphical parallel comes from Gortyn in Crete, but is considerably earlier as it dates to the 5th century B. C.[121] In this inscription, the property is confiscated from a house, which apparently did not belong to the offender or simply he did not live there. The burden of proof, however, was on its supposed legal owner who could retain his property by producing witnesses who would have to testify in his favor, or better to swear an oath on his behalf. This is not a clear-cut parallel, but in both cases the confusion over the identity of the offender whose property must be repossessed finds a remedy in the sworn testimony of a witness.

In Pergamon, if the repossessed goods were not claimed within five days, they were sold at an auction that had to take place ἢ ἐν φράτρηι ἢ ἐν τῆι ἀγορᾶ̣ πληθυούσῃ,[122] which are hard for us to explain as locations. Klaffenbach attempted an explanation for *phratry* following Hitzig: "(der Zweck ist offensichtlich der,) die Sache tunlichst der Famile zu erhalten."[123] This too is rather an obscure statement and in any case it cannot be in any way supported if only because this is the only attestation of phratries in Pergamon. In other words, we only know that these existed, but the role they played in the social and administrative structure of Pergamon is utterly unknown and speculating would be fruitless. Be that as it may, we should acknowledge the fact that the *astynomoi* had to be present at the auction of which the *amphodarchai* were in charge. The money of the sale had to be handed over to no longer attested magistrates.

Although the text offers some interesting details on the procedure regulating the confiscation – or better a seizure as security – and the

practice that we know from demotic documents that in their Greek translation use the same term, but refer to a different type of oath.

120 See the discussion by Hitzig 1905, 432–436, see also idem, 1905 *Nachtrag*.

121 See *I.Cr.* IV. 81, LL. 16–23: . . *vac.* κ' αἴ κ' ἐς στέγα/ς ἐνεχυράκσōντι, πōνίον[τι μ]/[ὲ 'νϝ]οικε͂ν ọ̔ ἐνεχύρακσαν συν/εκσομόσαθθαι τõν ὀμό[ρōν] (20) [τõ]ν ἐννέα τρίινς, οἷς κα προ/ϝείπε͂ι, μὲ ἐνϝοικẹṿ ὃ ἐνεχύ[ρα]/[κσ]α[ν· *vac* α]ὶ δὲ τίς καί τõν ὀμόρ/ōν. "If they confiscate (?) from a house and the one who has suffered the repossession claims not to live in the house, three of the nine neighbors whom he has named must swear that he does not live in the house where they confiscated". See Koerner 1993, n. 155. Latte 1920, p. 13; Hitzig 1905, p. 483. Oaths were used routinely to clear situations and even officials, see for example *IG* IX 2. 1109.I esp. LL. 58–61; see also Saba 2010, esp. pp. 296–298.

122 See Seyfarth 1955, pp. 29–33.

123 Klaffenbach 1954, p. 14 cites Hitzig 1905, p. 440.

auction, several questions remain unanswered. For example, it is not known how long the offenders had been in contempt before their property was seized. Or it is equally unknown what would have happened if the rightful owner decided to buy the property again, if he could. While the general principles guiding the procedure are sufficiently clear, data is lacking that would allow contextualizing it in the chain of events that finally led to the auction and in which the public administration had a direct bearing.

4.4 Column III

The stone preserves almost entirely the third column that concerns the role the *astynomoi* had within the city's building policy. Of special interest are private housing and infrastructures that could have been of public use and utility.

Other *poleis* must have had equally detailed regulations, but in Pergamon, the need for such provisions must have been felt acutely because of the steep nature of the land on which the city was built, namely the flanks of a hill, while the plain around it was occupied only later.[124] Before analyzing the content of the column, it is profitable to look at the archeological findings for private dwellings and other possibly relevant structures in Pergamon so as to incorporate this data into the discussion of the epigraphic text.

In the last decades, domestic architecture has become an increasingly more popular field of research and, as far as Western Turkey is concerned, ongoing archeological activity may bring to light further evidence also from neighboring cities such as Atarneus, Aigai, or further south in Priene, which could help clarify the development of Hellenistic forms of habitation.[125] Until that day, however, the reference work for housing in Pergamon will be *AvP* XV.3 by U. Wulf on the excavated residential quarter. This volume must be approached with caution, as it has now been superseded in a few aspects.[126] In the secondary literature,

[124] See Hellmann 1999, p. 21.

[125] See the groundbreaking study by Hoepfner and Schwandner 1994 and the subsequent studies by Nevett 2005, 1999, 1995. On Elaia and Atarneus see Pirson 2007, pp. 42–58. On Priene see Raeck 2005, pp. 147–163.

[126] Radt started the exploration of part of the residential area of the city in the early 70s, – the reports in *AA* date to 1973 onwards –, but Wulf published the

the area under consideration is called *Wohnquartier*, although we do not know what such a territorial unit was called in Greek or whether it was perceived as a unit.[127] On the ground, this is located inside the circle of walls that Philetairos built in the 3rd century B. C. Two streets (Ost- and Mittelgasse) and the main road in town (Hauptstrasse) that goes uphill define its perimeter.[128] Houses have been excavated within it and show a complex stratigraphy indicating that they were inhabited continuously until the Byzantine period with due modifications. Because of these, only a few Hellenistic structures survive. Nevertheless, plans have been drawn and then compared with the findings from other sites leading to the conclusion that Pergamene houses had no unique plan, as is the case in Priene, Olynthus or Abdera.[129] Instead, in Pergamon several types of houses coexisted so that one can detect typical, but not repetitive plans.[130] The most common is the so-called courtyard house in both its sub-types: *prostas* and *pastas*.[131] Their plan could be arranged in different ways, but always includes an open space, colonnaded or not, that precedes the rooms. Houses were built extremely close to one another on the hillside and often had two floors, with the rooms upstairs receiving more light. The open space was paved and often had a cistern to collect pluvial water from the roof and the courtyard.[132] Wulf noted that this building pattern continues well into the Roman times, when houses were often modified and enlarged, although the unvaried dimensions of the plots did not allow for too radical changes. Fancy peristyle-houses were not common and, as a type, they are better represented by the more monumental buildings located in other areas of town.[133] These

final results only in 1999. To date, her interpretations and results are considered partly superseded, on which see the *AA* annual reports by F. Pirson. I confine my reference to the actual data recorded in *AvP* XV 3.

127 See *supra* my comment on LL. 48–65.

128 Wulf 1999, pp. 1–3.

129 But see Raeck 2005, p. 152.

130 See Wulf 1999, pp. 187–190. For a general treatment of possible 'causes' for the coexistence of different plans see Aylward 2005, esp. p. 49 whose main focus is the Troad, although he presents numerous *comparanda*.

131 A definition in Nevett 2005, p. 3.

132 Cisterns are very common, but several houses also had pipes that brought water directly from the Madradag aqueduct, which allows dating them to the reign of Eumenes' II. See Wulf 1999, p. 21.

133 Excavations have revealed monumental private buildings, such as building Z, "Attalos' Hause" and several peristyle houses, in the lower part of the city, by the

would indeed have needed bigger lots than those available in the area under consideration. Their rooms could be arranged following either an U-shaped plan, *i. e.* with rooms on three sides of the peristyle, or a L-shaped, with rooms on two sides. An example of an elaborate peristyle house is Attalos' House by the lower Agora. It is called after its owner Attalos Paterklianos who lived around A. D. 200 and it underwent several construction phases, but still preserves mosaics that date to the Hellenistic Period.[134] In the residential quarter, however, examples of "small" peristyle houses are attested too, which only goes to prove that in Pergamon a variety of structures and plans coexisted.[135]

This is a very brief summary of the extensive work that has been done on housing in this town, but it is enough to grasp the details that the regulation provides for the physical maintenance of local private buildings.

LL.103–105: The grammatical subject of the first two verbs attested on stone is lost, but was certainly different from that (οἱ κεκτημένοι) of the third verb. The most likely hypothesis is that it was a board of magistrates, possibly the *astynomoi*, but there is no certainty that this was the case.[136] The text prescribes that these officials carry out an inspection (ἐπισκοπείτωσαν) of no longer specified structures and stipulates that a negative judgment on their solidity would mean that their owners had to restore them. What these structures were exactly is unclear and has been the subject of a scholarly debate. The question is whether these lines are already concerned with the κοινοὶ τοῖχοι that the text discusses later. Klaffenbach already concluded that this must have

---

Lower Agora and Gymnasium. The findings suggest that they had first been built in the Hellenistic period (or even earlier) and often modified, usually enlarged, during the Roman period. There are traces of material earlier than the 3rd B. C., but their structure cannot be recovered. See Radt 1999(a), pp. 119–127 for a summary, an exhaustive study in Pinkwart and Stammnitz, *AvP* XIV, 1984, esp. pp. 2–77.

134 Radt 1999(a), pp. 120–124 and p. 370 with further bibliographical references.

135 See for example Wulf 1999, pp. 119–134. Komplex X; briefly also Saliou 1994, pp. 103–107. On the two types of peristyle houses, L and U plan, see Pinkwart and Stammnitz 1984, Zusammenfassung.

136 See already Kolbe 1902, p. 66. Restorations should in my opinion be avoided since throughout the inscription several boards appear and often the subject changes unexpectedly.

been the case[137] and, I add, this becomes apparent in LL. 105–106 since these record that the complaint triggering the inspection came from one of two owners. The object of the inspection was then shared between two people, as for example common walls are.

LL. 105–108: LL. 106–107 record the presence of a damaged party. Possibly this party protested formally to the authorities who then inspected the infrastructure, LL. 103–104. The provisions that follow regulate the boards' behavior when faced with the second party's refusal to repair the property that had caused the damage. The officials in charge are the *astynomoi* who must assign the restoration job to contractors. In this case, however, the text seems to say that they could act together with one of those who had been wronged.[138] In the apodosis of the conditional clause, this is described as τοῦ προαιρουμένου τῶν βλαπτομένων, which has caused some discussion. Kolbe understood the idiom as "Vertreter der Geschädigten," but Dittenberger, Keil and Klaffenbach preferred to read the expression as "mit demjenigen der Geschädigten, der will,"[139] namely the party willing to cooperate. This must be right, since the participle προαιρουμένου reproduces the meaning of a προαίρησις or choice. More importantly, the subsequent sentence shows the involvement of two people only, one of whom had to pay 2/5 of the damages that had occurred. This means that there was no need of a representative, since technically only one person had suffered damage.[140]

LL.108–112: This sentence specifies the share that the two parties involved had to pay thus providing additional clues on the topic of these lines. The regulation imposes that the one who did not 'obey' pays 3/5 of the total costs, while τοῦ ἄλλου is responsible for the rest of the amount.[141] This clarifies that two neighbors shared the damaged structure and that one of them did not want to pay the cost of the restoration alone, for which he thought he was not responsible, either at all or at

[137] Klaffenbach 1954, p. 14.

[138] The verb has already appeared in restoration in col. I, LL. 52–54 where (the *astyno*[*moi*) ἐκδότωσαν μετὰ τοῦ ἀ]μφοδάρχου. On *ekdosis* see *supra* LL. 7–14.

[139] Klaffenbach 1954, p. 15.

[140] More recently, Hellmann 1999, p. 19 has translated the passage as follows: "une des personnes lésées, choisie par eaux."

[141] For fractions see Klaffenbach 1954, p. 15. Possibly, this was also τοῦ προαιρουμένου τῶν βλαπτομένων of LL. 107–108.

least not alone. It is for this reason that the damaged (?) owner made sure that the authories were involved and would intervene to force the other (unwilling) party to contribute to the expenses.

LL.112–123: Syntactically, this section opens with a genitive absolute followed by three conditional clauses. These establish the amount of money that each resident owed for the repair of common walls that function as the subject of the genitive absolute. What is noteworthy is how the due sum varies according to how houses were built and their location in relation to each other.

The genitive absolute sets the tone of the whole paragraph by firmly establishing the main issue: common walls. As briefly reported, the excavation of the residential quarter in Pergamon has revealed that this was a densely populated and built-up area, with houses constricted into well-delimited spaces. The law conveys exactly the same impression on the organization of the urban space. Reading the text, one imagines a crowded residential area constructed on steep ground where unstable common walls and freely flowing water could be a serious threat to the surrounding structures. To these problems remedies had to be found, provisions had to be passed and implemented. Finally, as the law clarifies, the difficulty of maintaining these structures also depended on the fact that many walls were shared and the two parties were not always in agreement. If we admit that LL. 103–112 are all concerned with common walls, we must assume that not every owner was willing to spend money on the necessary repairs, which eventually triggered the intervention of the authorities. A fair assumption is that this must have been a recurrent problem given that the law contained an *ad hoc* provision. Be that as it may, once it had been established that the walls had to be repaired LL. 112–123 explain how the financial burden was to be shared. The main criterion to determine the amount due was the arrangement of the houses on the ground. If two houses shared walls "in the same way," *i. e.* both or neither abutting, the repair costs had to be divided equally between owners. But if one of the houses leaned against a common wall, which only marked the limit of the neighbor's courtyard, then the owner of the first house had to pay a larger share, more precisely two-thirds against one third. Finally, the subsequent clause establishes that this principle applied also to the number of floors and owners of a one-floor-house paid the lesser amount, if the neighbor had two floors.

Let us consider for a moment together regulation, excavations and the stratified chronology, that is to say the excavated houses preserve traces of reuse up to the Roman period, often within the same constrained spaces, despite remodeling. The layout and the problems depending on space and neighboring issues cannot have changed through the centuries. This in turn suggests that the hypothesis that provisions passed in the 2nd century B. C. were still applicable three centuries later is not at all far-fetched. Housing policy may not be sufficient proof for the continuous applicability of the law in imperial time, but the point must be made and is of moderate importance given the nature of this law.

LL.123–128: General provisions on the legal and financial responsibilities pertaining to common walls precede the description of the procedure to be followed against those who actually damaged them. The *astynomoi* shall receive the formal accusation against the perpetrator who, if found guilty of the misdeed, would have to pay for the damages. The inscription uses a specific legal vocabulary here and describes the procedure as πρόσκλησις.[142] Also, it establishes a monetary punishment once the defendants have been found guilty, as the expression κρίσει νικηθέντες explains. The *astynomoi* had to register the accusation against the perpetrator, but it is not clear whether they were also in charge of the final decision, which possibly would mean that they had some form of judicial capacity (?). This question is, however, better left open for now.

LL.128–132: provide another list of illegal activities perpetrated against common walls that authorities had to try to prevent. Nobody was allowed to build on or by, to dig under or by, or to cut through the walls without the owner(s)' consent. These are fairly standard measures and are also partly paralleled in the well-known *P.Hal.* 1 that dates to the mid of the 3rd century B. C.[143] This papyrus was first published in 1913 and contains prescriptions on very different problems, which has led scholars

[142] See BERNEKER, *RE* XXIII, I 1957 col. 849–856. See also *Ath. Pol.* 29.4 on which RHODES 1981, p. 378 defining *prosklesis* as "the prosecutor's summons to a defendant to appear before the relevant magistrates."

[143] See *Dikaiomata* 1913, pp. 15–24; and see also *infra*, p. 112.

to assume that the different paragraphs collected there are excerpts from several documents that an attorney assembled at some point. The second section of the papyrus, LL. 79–114, records part of a πολιτικὸς νόμος possibly from Alexandria, which, as the first commentators noted, is a Greek law meant to regulate the everyday life of the *polis*. A few provisions appear to discipline the planting of trees, building of new structures and digging of ditches, while a second section treats the digging of trenches and their cleaning, thus constituting a parallel to our text.[144] From the point of view of the history of legal issues, another noteworthy aspect is the similarity of these lines with the Solonian law that Gaius cites in reference to the planting of trees.[145] Early Attic law actually influenced Hellenistic legislation, especially in relation to themes that were of no political consequence, such as for example neighbors' rights. Such matters return, quite logically, in a text like the Astynomoi law that could then be thought of as applicable to almost any society throughout the centuries.

LL.132–135: after 'common walls,' the text moves on to address the problems that could arise from other types of walls and more specifically from the so-called τοῖχοι πρόσχωροι. By definition these should delimit private property, but are not shared between owners. Interestingly, this section does not describe problems at length, rather envisions a possible, technical solution in the construction of the *peristasis* (ditch) to damages that humidity could cause. According to the text, a *peristasis* could be built only if the deviser had free, unoccupied space bordering on the neighbor's property, or, in Greek, αὐτοῖς οἱ κύριοι ὑπαίθροις οὖσιν τὰ πρὸς τοὺς γείτονας. By accepting this reading, I follow Klaffenbach for whom: "wir müssen wissen, daß die Mauern nach der Nachbarseite hin freistehend sind, daß wir es hier also mit einer ähnlichen Situation zu tun haben wie in Z. 117/8." [146]

---

144 See *Dikaiomata* 1913, pp. 64–76.

145 See *infra* comment to LL. 159–163.

146 With this reading there is no need to tamper with the article τά found on the stone. In the past, the article was emended to become an accusative, feminine plural to agree with περιστάσεις. See also KLAFFENBACH 1954, p. 16.

LL.134–144: The standard definition of *peristasis* is that of a space between a wall of a temple's cella and the outer columns.[147] In the Astynomoi law, however, the meaning has to be different if only because it deals with civil, not sacred architecture. For this reason I assume that here *peristasis* indicates the space between two properties that do not share a wall.

Pergamon was built on a slope, which caused many of the houses to stand at different levels. This must have had consequences for the drainage of water, which threatened major damages to houses located on lower levels.[148] Clearly *peristaseis* could help put a stop to this and the text specifies that they were built to lessen the deleterious effects that the geomorphological nature of Pergamon's location had on buildings. Here, I propose exploring how a *peristasis* was built, with which materials and in which spaces; in brief, what a *peristasis* was. I prefer to retain the Greek word, but its translations could help readers to familiarize themselves with it. Among the several – and multilingual – suggestions, I report those I find to be the most meaningful, such as for example the German *Isoliergang,* or the French *galerie sanitaire.* Also, one important detail pertains to the parallel between the Greek *peristasis* and the Roman *ambitus* that scholars have proposed in the past; so far the theory.

In 1902, Kolbe had well understood and shown the nature of this infrastructure by providing an explanatory sketch (see Fig. 3), which represents the reality of the lay-out, as later excavations have revealed.[149] According to the inscription, the *peristasis* is a ditch dug along the wall of a house located at a lower level, but could be built only if free space (a courtyard) was available on the higher level. The ditch was not supposed to be wider than one cubit and had to be covered with stone copings. The text then recommends that the external wall be built securely, if there was no bedrock on which copings could be laid.[150] The next sentence

---

[147] See KOLBE 1902, p. 68: "den Gang, der zwischen der Cellawand und der äusseren Säulenstellung bleibt". Or see also the note to L. 90 in *Syll.*[3] 972: "(peristasis) ea stylobatae pars, quae inter columnas et parietem cellae sita est".

[148] See also HELLMANN 1999, p. 21.

[149] Among the many references that can be provided, see WULF 1999, pp. 11 and PINKWART and STAMMNITZ 1984, p. 41.

[150] L. 141 contains the hardly justifiable noun πέτραι. KLAFFENBACH 1954, p. 16 retained it as it appears on stone following Keil who thought it represented an *Anticipation des Ortsbegriffes*: "wo der Dativ κατὰ σύνεσιν zu dem ἐπι- in dem

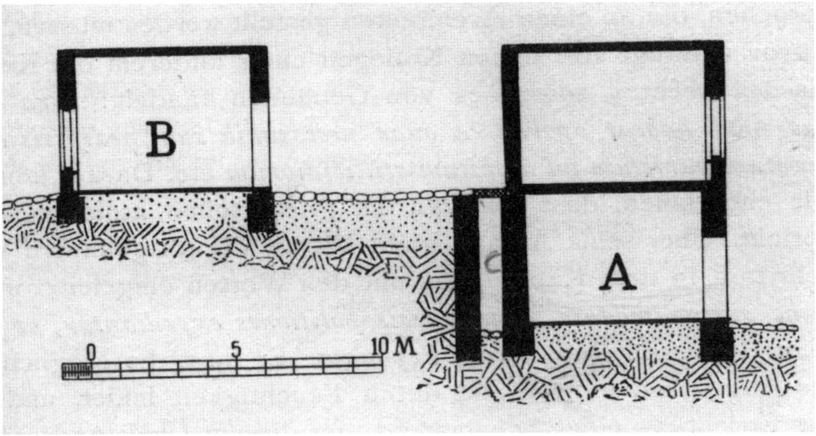

Fig. 3: Sketch of the *peristasis* by W. Kolbe, "Die Arbeiten zu Pergamon 1900–1901; Die Astynomeninschrift," *AM* 1902, pp. 47 – 77, esp. p. 69. Courtesy of the DAI, Istanbul.

provides additional instructions by stating that the 'floor' must not be higher than the courtyard, lest the water should not flow properly.[151] This last point clarifies the main function of these infrastructures: they were built mainly to protect walls from water and the damages caused by wetness.

The Pergamon excavation has substantiated Kolbe's reconstruction with the discovery of numerous ditches. In her 1999 work, Wulf describes a *peristasis* as follows: "(A *peristasis*) ist mit wasserundurchlässigem Ziegelsplittmörtel ausgekleidet. Die Isoliergänge waren, wie dies noch in situ befindliche Platte der Peristasis nordwestich des Raumes XI, 4 zeigt, und wie es auch in der Astynomeninschrift beschrieben ist, mit Andesitplatten abgedeckt."[152] These *peristaseis* collected water that was conveyed into channels and, when possible, into a central *hyponomos* to be redistributed and reused.[153] Also, several ditches were found still covered

Verb konstruiert ist." I still prefer to expunge the final i thus turning the dative into a nominative.

151 See also *OGIS* 483 n. 52 for a comment on the language.

152 Wulf 1999, p. 11.

153 See Wulf 1999, p. 23. For example on the Ostgasse she says: "In diesen Abwasserkanal münden an beiden Seiten der Gassen kleinere, 20–30 cm breite Kanäle, über die das Wasser, der die einzelne Gebäude voneinander abgrenzen-

with stone copings. According to Wulf, however, not all the excavated houses had *peristaseis* and apparently, by the 2nd A. D. they were filled in and no longer in use. In this regard, the comparison between Greek *peristasis* and Roman *ambitus*,[154] which followed the same principles structurally, is relevant. The *ambitus* disappeared in the early empire already, but in the section devoted to the Great Fire of Rome during Nero's reign, Tacitus states: *et subsidia reprimendis ignibus in propatulo quisque haberet, nec communione parietum, sed propriis quaeque muris ambirentur.*[155] The historian thus testifies to an attempt on the part of the emperor to re-introduce the *ambitus* by prohibiting common walls and encouraging separate ones with an intermediate space between them.[156] Nero's attempt was unsuccessful, but this does not mean that he was the last to acknowledge the utility of this intramural space.

I have already mentioned Wulf's observation on the progressive abandonment of *peristasis* in Pergamon on which one can speculate. If this *prostagma* was still applicable in the 2nd century A. D., the lines concerning the *peristasis* might have implied a last attempt to revitalize its use by regulating construction and proper maintenance: whether this was succesful or not is of no consequence here. What matters is that this could have been an attempt to bring this structure back into use. Be that as it may, *peristaseis* must have been fairly common in Greek cities during the Hellenistic age, as a simple walk through the remains of Ephesos or Priene shows. For example, an inscription from Ephesos mentions a similar structure, but in reference to fortifications where the term must indicate a space around the walls; again this was a different use of the same structure and possibly to the same end.[157] The Astynomoi

den Peristasen in den grossen Sammelkanal geleitet werde". Hauptstrasse and Ostgasse have *hyponomoi*, but not the Mittelgasse where the water coming from roofs runs into a water deposit.

154 Three sources provide a definition: VARRO, *De ling. Lat.* V. 22; VITRUV. I.1.10, and *C.J.C.* VIII.12.2. See BRUGI 1887.

155 TAC. *Ann.* 15.43. The goal of this intramural space seems that of hindering fire from spreading, in the same section, however Tacitus also says that: *"erant tamen qui crederent veterem illam formam salubritati magis conduxisse, quoniam angustiae itinerum et altitudo tectorum non perinde solis vapore perrumperentur"*

156 ZACCARIA-RUGGIU 1990, p. 81 says: "il progetto urbanistico neroniano di Roma, può considerarsi l'ultima pianificazione in cui questo tipo di spazio, peraltro documentato solo dalla testimonianza letteraria, venga imposto."

157 *I. Ephesos* 3, LL. 5–6.

law clearly only describes a potentially common solution for a common problem.

LL.144–148: The regulation provides additional indications on the legal status and ownership of a *peristasis*. According to these lines, a *peristasis* belongs to the builder even if it physically lies on the neighbor's ground, once it has been covered with stone copings. The neighbor can use the *peristasis*, but only as long as this does not damage the other resident's walls.

LL.149–155: The next 6 lines deal with technicalities related to the maintenance of the *peristasis*. This had to be accessible for cleaning and repairs from the owner's house,[158] provided that the *astynomoi* and the city architect determined that this was possible. If they decided against this, then the neighbors had to grant entrance to the *peristasis*.

LL.156–159: the peculiar provision recorded in this part must be read in connection with the preceding lines. According to the text, if the *astynomoi* caught an intruder entering the *peristasis* with malicious intentions, the offender(s) had to be fined five drachmas.[159] The determination of the state of mind (malicious intent) of the perpetrator was the *astynomoi*'s task; also, they had to apprehend this individual in flagrant violation of the law. This, however, does not imply that they patrolled the city. Instead procedures similar to *ephegesis* in Athens must have existed in Pergamon and these allowed a third party to guide officials to where misdeeds were taking place.[160] If this was the case, any resident could report the offense and lead the magistrates to the scene of the crime.

LL.159–166: these lines virtually close a section of the third column, even if no genitive appears.

LL. 159–163 provide a brief list of illegal acts that could damage walls: residents shall not dig or plant anything by them. None of these measures is unusual however; for example, *D.* 10.1.13 cites a comment by Gaius

[158] On this see RADT 1994, p. 422.

[159] In L. 158 καταλάμβανω has the same meaning as καταδικάζω, see KLAFFENBACH 1954, p. 16.

[160] On *ephegesis* see HARRISON 1971, pp. 231–232.

on the XII Tables that recorded provisions on minimum distances to be respected when undertaking a construction or act that could be a threat to the integrity of others' property. Gaius stresses that this entry was modeled on Solon's *nomos*, which he also cites.[161] Finally, similar provisions are attested in *P.Hal.* 1, where the influence of Attic legislation on Hellenistic regulations is again visible.[162]

Just as it was to be expected, the last two lines of this passage concern the consequences that offenders had to face if caught and establish that the owner had to report the damages his wall suffered to the *astynomoi*. Quite exceptionally, the *astynomoi* must decide alone the most appropriate punishment/fine, if any. Such autonomy is attested possibly only one more time in the text, in the first lines of the inscription, Col. I, LL. 2–3, which are largely in lacuna.[163] The part still readable, however, namely . . . ι̣ δίχ̣αιον suggests that such restoration is probably accurate.

LL.166–170: the protasis of a conditional clause whose meaning can be guessed in spite of its fragmentary state closes the column. Neighbors had the right to intervene if the walls of a house close to their own showed signs of advanced decay and needed repair. These attentive citizens were to report this to the competent authorities which presumably were the *astynomoi*. Kolbe and Dittenberger restored the last line differently, Klaffenbach decided not to supplement the text at all. I took the latter's approach in my text since these lines are too fragmentary. Any restoration is strictly *exempli gratia*.[164]

---

161 *D.* 10.1.13: *GAIUS libro quarto ad legem duodecim tabularum.* Sciendum est in actione finium regundorum illud observandum esse, quod ad exemplum quodammodo eius legis scriptum est, quam Athenis Solonem dicitur tulisse: nam illic ita est: ἐάν τις αἱμασιὰν παρ' ἀλλοτρίῳ χωρίῳ ὀρύγῃ, τὸν ὅρον μὴ παραβαίνειν· ἐὰν τειχίον, πόδα ἀπολείπειν· ἐὰν δὲ οἴκημα, δὺο πόδας. ἐὰν δὲ τάφον ἢ βόθρον ὀρύττῃ, ὅσον τὸ βάθος ᾖ, τοσοῦτον ἀπολείπειν, ἐὰν δὲ φρέαρ, ὀργυιάν. ἐλαίαν δὲ καὶ συκῆν ἐννέα πόδας ἀπὸ τοῦ ἀλλοτρίου φυτεύειν, τὰ δὲ ἄλλα δένδρα πέντε πόδας. See RUSCHENBUSCH 1966, esp. 91–92.

162 See *supra* LL. 128–132.

163 [- - ἐπισκοπείτωσαν καὶ ἐπικρεινέτ]ω/[σαν, καθ' ἃ ἄν αὐτοῖς φαίνητα]ι̣ δίχ̣αιον / [εἶναι . . .

164 On the dangers of too readily accepted restorations see BADIAN 1989, pp. 59–70.

4.5 Column IV

A general, yet true statement is that water was a concern in the ancient world, just as much as it is today. This section of the Astynomoi law only confirms this. When it comes to water supplies, it is customary to find that Roman interventions improved the condition of many cities that became part of her empire.[165] Pergamon, however, was well served already in Hellenistic time, *i. e.* under the Attalids, with its three aqueducts. Nonetheless, fountains, and above all cisterns were numerous and were probably among the most important water infrastructures that this *polis* used to provide (drinking)-water to its residents. Both had to be properly maintained and their state closely monitored.

Another important aspect for water administration concerns the magistrates in charge of it. The Aristotelian *Athenaion Politeia* asserts that in Athens the officials responsible for the local fountains were among the few to be elected instead of being chosen by lot, as customary.[166] In the *Politics,* Aristotle states that populous cities had *ad hoc* officials supervising fountains and Plato in the *Laws* affirms that the *astynomoi*, who are elected, were responsible for assuring that the town of Magnesia was properly provided for with water.[167] Finally, the Messenian Andania law records that during celebrations it was for the *agoranomos* together with the περὶ τοῦ ὕδατος to be in charge of local water sources, L. 106, who must have had specific competences.[168] This very brief overview of some of the available evidence on water administrators already indicates that such offices were trusted to the care of skilled, experienced men and were not left to chance, not even in democratic Athens. Most likely this was true for Pergamon too where we know that *astynomoi* had supervisory duties on water sources. Inferences on their mode of appointment are risky as no evidence whatsoever survives on this, but candidates for

---

165 See Boatwright's 2000 last chapters on Hadrian's interventions. She offers illuminating comments on his predecessor(s) and occasionally successors' activity.

166 *Ath. Pol.* 43, 1: τὰς δ' ἀρχὰς τὰς περὶ τὴν ἐγκύκλιον διοίκησιν ἁπάσας ποιοῦσι κληρωτάς, πλὴν ταμίου στρατιωτικῶν καὶ τῶν ἐπὶ τῶν θεωρικῶν καὶ τοῦ τῶν κρηνῶν ἐπιμελητοῦ. ταύτας δὲ χειροτονοῦσιν. On this passage Rhodes 1981, pp. 516–517; Habicht 1989, p. 84.

167 Arist. *Pol.* VIII, 1321b, 23–27; Pl. *Leg.* 763c.

168 *LSCG* 65, now see also Deshours 2006, p. 39–40.

the office must have had some qualification before being invested with it given the responsibility it entailed.

L.171: The first line of the fourth and last column of the Astynomoi law preserves only the last few letters of ἀναγκάζω followed by an infinitive, ἐκκαθαίρειν. A good part of the sentence is lost but its gist must presumably be that a board, perhaps that of the *astynomoi*,[169] had to force residents (?) to clean the *hyponomoi* that are the object of the infinitive.[170] The object of the provisions listed in this column is already clear: the city aimed to regulate the behavior of residents in their use of local water infrastructures through the activity of the *astynomoi*.

Since the general context is lost, we are not informed of the specific function of these *hyponomoi*: fountains and latrines could use *hyponomoi*, but are discussed later in the text. Other inscriptions, however, may provide a clue such as for example *IG* XII. 9. 191 A also known as the Chaerephanes' text. This stone comes from Eretria and dates to a year between the end of the 4th and the beginning of the 3rd century B. C., according to D. Knoepfler's latest study on it.[171] Within the description of the procedure that Chaerephanes had to follow to drain a marsh, LL. 17–27 have been restored with a reference to *hyponomoi* connected to a well. In LL. 24–27 the inscription specifies that one of these conduits run into a cistern, which contained the water for irrigating the land that had been recovered from the drainage.[172] Stretching the connection a bit, we could hypothesize that *hyponomoi* were used in an irrigation system, which would hardly be of use in town unless there were urban gardens there, which is a possibility. More generally these *hyponomoi* were connected with wells, in what capacity we cannot say.

---

169 On this restoration see Klingenberg 1979, p. 287.

170 For a definition of *hyponomoi* see *supra* the commentary to LL. 86–88.

171 Knoepfler 2001, p. 41 on the date, commentary pp. 41–80, see *supra* comment to LL. 86–88.

172 LL. 17–19: [. . . καὶ ἐξέστω δὲ Χαιρεφάνει κα]/[ὶ] ἐν τοῖς ἰδ̣ιωτικοῖς χωρίοις φρεατία[ς] ποιεῖν τῶ[ι ὑπονόμωι, ἀλλὰ ταύτας μὴ ποείτω πλὴν διὰ τοῦ χωρί]/ου οὗπερ καὶ πρότερον τὴν τιμὴν δῷ. LL. 24–25 καὶ δρυφάκτ[ους δὲ ποησάσθω περὶ τὴν δεξαμενήν· ἔνθα δὲ τὸ ὕδωρ εἰσπίπτει εἰς [τ]ὸν ὑπόνομον, καὶ θύραν ἐργασάσθω. See also Fantasia 1999, n. 142 who states that the word ὑπόνομος is aways associated with φρέας, and: "(Essi) ricompaiono accoppiati ogniqualvolta si tratta di scavare una conduttura sotterranea destinata a un qualsiasi scopo."

LL.172–176: the genitive κρηνῶν, *i. e.* fountains, introduces a new section from which we learn that the *astynomoi* were also in charge of supervising all fountains, in and outside town. Their main duty was to make sure that the *hyponomoi* used for the inflow and outflow of water were clean and never stopped up.

The intense archaeological activity that still continues in Pergamon has shown that this *polis* did not have many fountains.[173] Only a few are still preserved and scholarship classifies them according to two types. A monumental fountain that was located on the main street by the Mid- and Low Gymnasium best represents the first type. This is commonly known as the 'city-fountain' and dates to the first half of the 2nd century B. C. Columns and a marble head that must have been part of its decoration underline its monumentality, which is further confirmed by the capacity of 50 m^3 of the basin from which several pipes ran to the lower Agora. It is through these that the fountain collected the water that was then re-distributed in the lower city. The most common assumption is that one of the three Hellenistic aqueducts serviced it, but archaeological research has not yet found out which one it was.[174]

An example of the second 'type' is the so-called 'Fountain-house' in complex IX. Its remains are still visible in the southwest area of the residential quarter, on the main street, and show that it was an imposing building with several rooms and an internal basin.[175] A cistern served this complex, which was used continuously, with modifications, until the 2nd century A. D. It has been rightly pointed out too that these constructions were generally built at or by important crossways or on the way to sanctuaries or sacred areas.[176]

LL.176–180: In L. 180, the text specifies that the regulation applied to all public fountains and then focuses on their maintenance. If any fountain needed repair, the *astynomoi* (?) had to report to higher officials. These are the usual *strategoi*, but here they work with the official in charge of sacred money, ὁ ἐπὶ τῶν ἱερῶν προσόδων who was another city official. This official is attested only three times for the Attalid King-

---

[173] See GARBRECHT 2001, p. 13 and WULF 1999, pp. 113 –117.
[174] See WULF 1999, p. 114; RADT 1999(a), p. 148–149.
[175] See WULF 1999, pp. 102–113.
[176] WULF 1999, p. 117.

dom: in the Astynomoi Law, in a document from Sardis conferring honors to the local ἐπὶ τῶν ἱερῶν προσόδων, a Sardian named Euxenos son of Menander, and, finally, an inscription from Magnesia mentions this office in the plural in a text concerned with the celebration of the festival for Artemis.[177] All known istances for the ἐπὶ τῶν ἱερῶν προσόδων date to the second half of the II century B. C.; furthermore, *SEG* XXXII 1237, L. 1 mentions either the 6th or the 9th year of the reign of what we now know must have been one of the last Attalid kings.[178] In light of this, it is possible that the creation of the office of the ἐπὶ τῶν ἱερῶν προσόδων under one of the last two – or the last – Attalid kings represents also a *terminus post quem* for the Astynomoi law.[179]

To go back to our text, in LL. 176–180 the *strategoi* and the ἐπὶ τῶν ἱερῶν προσόδων are responsible for assigning the repair jobs. In this case the common administration of money suggests that these 'city fountains' were sanctuaries, perhaps in the form of a Nymphaeum, or perhaps they were important because they were all located in the proximities of sacred areas. Any one of these hypotheses can help to explain how this official responsible for sacred money was involved.

LL.180–184: The regulation lists a number of quite common rules that the authorities must have established to avoid the pollution of public water. Nobody could water their livestock, or wash anything, whether clothes or objects, in a public fountain. Similar prescriptions are often found in regulations pertaining to sacred areas too. A good example is *LSCG* 152 from Cos dated to the 4th century B. C.[180] This text is

---

177 Hoz de Paz 1999, n. 5.26, LL. 4–6 (*SEG* XXXII 1237); *I. Magn.* 100, LL. 73–74. See also Herrmann 2004, pp. 277–285; Müller 2000, pp. 523–525.

178 The most likely candidates are Attalos II or Attalos III, see Müller 2000, pp. 519–525; Robert 1987 (*BCH* 106, 1982, p. 326), p. 324 dated the text to the end of the I century B. C., but a new document published by Malay – Nalbantouglou 1996, n. 1, later Müller 2000, pp. 519–542, allows moving the date back to the II century B. C., possibly under Attalos II or III.

179 Müller 2003, p. 425: "Wenn sich als zutreffend erweisen sollte, dass die Einrichtung des im folgendes genannten Amtes des ἐπὶ τῶν ἱερῶν προσόδων frühestens unter Attalos erfolgte (Müller and Wörrle 2002, 231 f. Anm. 194) stammt das Gesetz aus den letzten Jahrhunderten der Monarchie." It is highly likely that this office was originally Seleucid and was just absorbed in the Attalid administrative system.

180 LL. 4–9 εἰς δὲ τὰς/ κράνας τὰς ἐν τῶι ἱερῶι μὴ ἐξέ/στω μηθενὶ πέμμα μηθὲν ἐνβάλ/λειν μηδὲ ἄλλο μηθέν· εἰ δέ τις / κα ἐνβάλει, καθαράτω τὸ ἱερὸν / τᾶν Νυμφᾶν

concerned with the cleanness of the fountains within the local sanctuary and can be considered a term of comparison to the Astynomoi law. The greater difference between the two does not lie in the provisions to avoid pollution, but in the consequences for the offenders. In Cos, no punishment is listed, only the obligation to clean. In Pergamon offenders would not get off very lightly, but this may depend on the nature of the inscription. Be that as it may, that of Cos is not an isolated case; for example, *LSS* 50 from Delos dated to the 5th century B. C. shows the same concerns and light punishment, only fines.

LL.185–192: In comparison with the just cited regulations, which are, however, hardly representative of the wide range of possible punishments that inscriptions testify to, the Astynomoi law is rather severe although not unparalleled. For example, a text from Poiessa in Keos, *IG* XII.5.569 dated to the beginning of the 3rd century B. C. regulates the cleaning of fountain drains[181] that brought water to the sanctuary of Demetra and lists rather severe fines and punishments against offenders. LL. 5–8 for example establish that even the 'sons of free men' will be punished corporally.[182] I must stress again that these are only very few examples and are not meant to be exhaustive or particularly representative for any kind of attitude of a community towards offenders. The possible modes

ὡς νομίζεται. "Nobody is allowed to throw sacrificial food or anything else into the fountains located in the sanctuary. If anybody throws anything (into them), the sanctuary of the Nymphai shall be cleaned as it seems proper."

181 The term used to indicate the drain is ὀχετός.

182 In LL. 5–8 of *IG* XII.5.569 we can read: · ἐὰ]ν δέ τις ἢ λόηται ἢ πλύνει τι / ἐν ταῖς κρήναις, κύριος ἔστω ὁ ἐπιμ[ελ]ητὴς τὸν μὲν ἐλεύθερον ζη/μιῶν [ἄχρ]ι δέκα δραχμῶν, τοὺς δὲ π[αῖδα]ς τοὺ[ς ἐ]λευθέρους καὶ τοὺς οἰκέτας πληγαῖς κολάζων· στῆ[σ]αι δὲ καὶ στήλην πρὸς ταῖς / κρήναις ὅπου ἂν δοκεῖ τῆι βουλῆι ἐπίκαιρον εἶναι· "If anyone pollutes or washes anything in the fountains, the official in charge shall fine a free man ten drachmai, the free children and servants shall he punished with lashes. A stele shall be set by the fountains where it seems fit to the council." These lines show that *free paides* were corporally punished, which seems to contradict the general principle of punish corporally only those who were not free. Another parallel comes from the Law of Beroia, Face B, LL. 19–23, that dates to *ca.* 200–166 B. C. The (free) *paides*, *i. e.* age group, could be flogged too, esp. Face B LL. 21–23: κύριος δὲ ἔστω ὁ γυμνασίαρχος καὶ τῶν / παίδων τοὺς ἀτακτοῦντας μαστιγῶν καὶ τῶν παιδαγωγῶν, / ὅσοι ἂν μὴ ἐλεύθεροι ὦσιν, τοὺς δὲ ἐλεύθερους ζημίων· "(The gymnasiarch) is in charge of punishing those among the *paides* who misbehaved and the pedagoges who are not of free condition, those who are free shall be fined." See GAUTHIER-HATZOPOULOS 1993, pp. 72–76; this must mean that corporal punishments were not tolerated for adult free men.

of treatement by the authorities of those who committed such crimes and misused local infrastructures and resources are wide-ranging and widely attested to the point that a pattern cannot be determined.[183]

The punishments for the offenders in Pergamon appear in LL. 185–192 and the criterion that determines the severity of the penalty is legal status. This is a widely attested principle too as is shown among many others in *IG* XII.5, 569, *LSS* 53, and also the slightly more secular 'Agoranomic law', *IG* II^2 380, that dates to 320/19 B. C. show. The latter is a very often-cited text because it has been interpreted as if it recorded the temporary abolition of the *astynomoi*, on which I have some reservations to be discussed in the following.[184] Unfortunately, its last lines, 40–44, are very fragmentary; there figured a legal differentiation in administering penalties similar to that found in the Astynomoi law. Several restorations have been suggested, but we only know with certainty that the punishments were different for slaves than for free men.[185] The Astynomoi law, however, goes further and articulates the

[183] For a reflection on the wide range of punishments attested in 'sacred laws' see NAIDEN 2008, pp. 125–138, but see also the answer in the same volume, pp. 125–144 where DREHER poses a different basis for the discussion of this rather broad theme. On "dumping and littering" in sacred laws see LUPU 2005, p. 28 and NÉMETH 1997, pp. 21–30.

[184] See *infra* my discussion on the *astynomia* in Athens.

[185] See *IG* II^2 380, LL. 41–44. The offense was littering. Another parallel comes from *D.* 43 10, 2 where legal status determines again the punishment. If the culprit were a slave, he was flogged right away, while a free man would be remanded to the authority of the *astynomoi* for a fine. DEMOSTH., *Contra Andr.* XXII 55, asserts the importance of legal status to determine the severity of the punishment. καὶ μὴν εἰ θέλετε σκέψασθαι τί δοῦλον ἢ ἐλεύθερον εἶναι διαφέρει, τοῦτο μέγιστον ἂν εὕροιτε, ὅτι τοῖς μὲν δούλοις τὸ σῶμα τῶν ἀδικημάτων ἁπάντων ὑπεύθυνόν ἐστιν, τοῖς δ' ἐλευθέροις, κἂν τὰ μέγιστ' ἀτυχῶσιν, τοῦτό γ' ἔνεστι σῶσαι· εἰς χρήματα γὰρ τὴν δίκην περὶ τῶν πλείστων παρὰ τούτων προσήκει λαμβάνει. "Indeed, if you wanted to point out the difference between the slave and the free man, you would find the most important distinction in the fact that slaves are responsible in person for all offenses, while free men, even in the most unfortunate circumstances, can protect their body. For indeed in the majority of cases it is with money that satisfaction is obtained." The orator clearly says that free men and slaves face different punishments: slaves will be punished corporally, while decency demands that this does not happen to free men, no matter what the charge is. See also NACHTERGAEL 1972, pp. 195–203 who comments on a fragmentary papyrus (*P. Brux.* Inv. E. 7172) dated to the 1st–2nd century A. D. of unknown provenance where provisions appear against a slave who is to be flogged. In L. 15 of the text ΑΣΤΥΝΟΜΟ are cited. Nachtergael stresses that this differentiation was the norm and cites other important parallels, for example *P. Hal.* 1, LL. 196–200,

punishments for slaves in an unusual way.[186] The penalty changes according to whether the slave acted on his own initiative or with his owner's consent. According to Klingenberg "è la regola in Grecia che soltanto il padrone venga ritenuto colpevole se lo schiavo commette un reato dietro suo ordine."[187] In the Astynomoi law, the slave is condemned to be flogged more or less severely depending on his master's involvement, thus adhering to this social-behavioral pattern, while the possible novelty lies in the expropriation of goods. If the owner was aware of the slave's action, the slave is deprived of the misused property. If the slave alone is responsible, the parenthetical sentence in L. 192, ὧν μὲν ἂν ἔχῃ, describes what shall be taken from the slave. Klaffenbach stressed the ambiguity of the clause and explained that it can mean that the slave is deprived of what he has, *i. e.* his belongings, or what he has brought to/from the fountain.[188] He opts for the second alternative, contradicting earlier scholarship, best represented by Hitzig, who asserted that only the slave's belongings were sequestered.[189] This apparently contradicts the basic principle that Klingenberg has formulated on the responsibility of the owner[190] and, if we admit that this applies to the Astynomoi law, then we are forced to assume that the owner's goods had to be confiscated. Also, the flogging should be seen as a punishment for the owner, too, as the slave was his property. As for the goods of which the slave is deprived, if he acted with the knowledge of the owner, Klaffenbach has suggested that these are again the things which he brought to the

the Astynomoi and the Andania Law, on which see HARTER – UIBOPUU 2002, esp. p. 147.

186 On slavery in Classical Athens see COHEN 2000; GAGARIN 1996. Hellenistic slavery has not been studied so fully, but see HEINEN 1976 and more recently BUSSI 2001.

187 See KLINGENBERG 1979, p. 289.

188 See KLAFFENBACH 1954, pp. 16–17.

189 HITZIG 1905, p. 446: "Hat der Sklave ohne Geheiß des Herrn in unerlaubter weise die Quelle benutzt, so verliert er, was er hat (ὧν μὲν ἂν ἔχῃ, [σ]τερήσθω), womit wohl nicht Vieh und Gerät des Herrn, sondern das eigene Vermögen des Sklaven gemeint ist."

190 On this principle see also HARTER-UIBOPUU 2002, pp. 145–147 on the Andania law.

fountain.[191] The punishment for the slave can be lighter or heavier, but as Klingenberg said the owner is responsible in any case.

LL.193–196: The inscription provides details on the means, ξύλον and κύφων, used to physically detain those who had been arrested. The use of two terms leads me to think that they must have been different from one another.[192] In *OGIS*, Dittenberger briefly reviewed the meaning of these nouns and specified that while the first, *kyphon,* was probably set around the neck of the offender, the second, *xyla,* was a device meant to constrain his feet.[193] If Dittenberger is right, the punishment was certainly meant to be humiliating. The prisoner was bound to the pillory (*kyphon*) "just" for the time of the flogging, while he was held in for ten days in shackles (*xyla*?). Our knowledge of the means of detention and/or torture, however, is incomplete. The term ξύλον indicates in truth a variety of detention instruments and late sources often use it as general term.[194] The immediate consequence of this linguistic simplification is that we cannot know what punishments the Astynomoi law imposed on the offenders. According to how ξύλον is interpreted for example, the final whipping could have been the more clement act.

LL.196–202: The Astynomoi law continues with a short section on personal initiative of residents against offenders who they witnessed defiling public fountains. According to the law, ὁ βουλόμενος[195] had the right of ἐπίληψις, which in very simple terms can be described as claiming property by seizing it from whoever is caught acting illegally here

191 Klaffenbach 1954, p. 17 points out that LL. 199–200 strengthen his position and asserts: "So kann ich in der Wendung ὧν μὲν ἄν ἔχῃ, [σ]τερήσθω nur das Bestreben sehen, sich nicht noch einmal der soeben gebrauchten Wendung ὁμοιως στερήσθω (Z. 189) zu bedienen." I am not sure *variatio* was a great concern to those who compiled this law.

192 So *OGIS* 483 n. 67: "hic titulus docet, κύφωνες et ξύλον, quae fuerunt qui confunderent, res diversas fuisse".

193 See *OGIS* 483 n. 66 and 67. Dittenberger reports many sources confirming this; see also the entry of the Suda for κύφωνες. See also Klingenberg 1979, p. 297, n. 91.

194 For an overview on these means of torture see Halm-Tisserant 1999, pp. 78–88. For the use of generic terminology already in the 5th century see Lys., *In Theomn.* 1, X, 16 citing a law by Solon: "ΝΟΜΟΣ· δεδέσθαι δ' ἐν τῇ ποδοκάκκῃ ἡμέρας πέντε τὸν πόδα, ἐὰν [μὴ] προστιμήσῃ ἡ ἡλιαία." Ἡ ποδοκάκκη αὕτη ἐστίν, ὦ Θεόμνηστε, ὃ νῦν καλεῖτε ἐν τῷ ξύλῳ δεδέσθαι.

195 On volunteer prosecutors see Rubinstein 2003, pp. 87–113.

to the detriment of public fountains.[196] According to the text, the person willing to make the ἐπίληψις of the culprits could either report to the *astynomoi* or bring them the offender (and?) with what he had, τὰ ληφθέντα. The award was half of what was made out of what he seized, while the other half was to be used for the maintenance of the Nymphs' sanctuary, which has not yet been located.[197] Seizure left to private initiative is a well-attested legal procedure, just to cite one example, *LSS* 53 LL. 15–20 dated to 202 B. C. from Delos states that half of what the offender has paid as a fine, if he is a free man, is to be given to the person who brought the misdeed to public attention, while the other half was to be handed to the sacred officials.

L.203: The genitive φρεάτων introduces the next to the last section. This noun normally means "well," but in this document signifies "cistern" and is used as a synonym for δεξαμενή.[198] The linguistic conflation might have depended on the fact that these two types of water deposits were respectively poorly and extremely well represented in town, or in other words, one term absorbed the other.

Cisterns were numerous in Pergamon. As of today, 149 of them have been located on the hilltop, in the residential quarter, and in the lower part of the city. For the most part they were built in the courtyard of houses and were dug in the ground with a cylindrical form and a depth ranging from 3 up to 15 m. This implies that their capacity varies as well. For example, some cisterns can contain 11 m^3 of water, while others have a capacity up to 53 m^3.[199] These collected pluvial water that was

---

[196] A similar use of the word in Pl. *Leg.* 954e.

[197] Radt 1999(a), p. 92. See also Ohlemutz 1968^2, pp. 244–250 who wanted to identify this with a structure he called a Nymphaeum in the area of the lower Agora. This identification has some credibility and also Radt suggested it, but only as a working hypothesis. Radt stressed indeed that this does not stand on a very solid foundation because of the paucity of surrounding water reservoirs that would have been necessary to the cult. Ohlemutz too had observed that the citation of this sanctuary in the fourth column of the law that is devoted to water was not casual.

[198] See Garbrecht 2001, pp. 23–36 and Klaffenbach 1954, p. 17.

[199] Garbrecht 2001, pp. 16–21. Brinker analyzed Pergamon's cisterns in his 1990 dissertation and several articles, among which Brinker 1986 where he discusses the Astynomoi law too. The data from new excavations does not alter the value of his work, but for a more recent overview see Garbrecht 2001 pp. 17–37 and Wulf 1999, pp. 20– 22.

channeled into them from roofs through open or closed conduits; also, they were paved and plastered with waterproof mortar.[200] It is hard to say whether they alone could have provided enough water for the whole city in any given period of time, especially since the number of the inhabitants is extremely difficult to determine. For antiquity, demographic studies can only make use of a very small set of data, which makes density and size of population always difficult to estimate.[201] Numbers have been suggested for Pergamon but with great uncertainty. For example, for the period under Eumenes II, it has been said that the *polis* had between 25.000 and 35.000 inhabitants. This figure should have increased rapidly throughout the centuries.[202] Even if we confine ourselves to the numbers given for the Hellenistic period, we must note that the difference between them is not negligible. Still if the data in our possession were even merely close to what they were in reality, it is likely that for a time cisterns were, at the very least, one of the main water reservoir-resources.

Garbrecht pointed out that the Astynomoi law does not preserve any prescription on building new cisterns, but only on maintaining old ones in the 2nd century B. C. By the 2nd century A. D., the many aqueducts built around town must have made these cisterns if not obsolete, at the very least, not the primary water source. This seems to be generally confirmed by the archaeological data. Apparently, several houses in the residential 'quarter' stopped using cisterns already in the late Hellenistic period and started employing running water brought by a piping system that ultimately must have been connected to aqueducts.

---

200 For the types of mortar available in Pergamon see GARBRECHT 2001, p. 25.

201 See SCHEIDEL 2009, pp. 134–145.

202 GARBRECHT 2001, p. 40, esp. n. 74 and BELOCH 1886, pp. 235–236 reporting the data provided by a passage of Galenus, *Aff. Dig.* V, 49. According to this, in the period of the Antonini, Pergamon had 120,000 inhabitants, among whom 40,000 were adult male and citizens. This, however, is only Galenus' estimate and was based on sources unknown (to us), if any. The numbers raise legitimate doubts mainly because of the nature of the writing and the context in which the remark is made. Indeed, this text deals with emotions, as the title suggests too, viz. in English "*The Passions of the Soul*", and the passage in question belongs to section on the constant state of dissatisfaction of man. To prove the correctness of his thesis the author says: εἴπερ οὖν ἡμῖν οἱ πολῖται πρὸς τοὺς τετρακισμυρίους εἰσίν, ὁμοῦ ἐὰν προσθῇς αὐτῶν τὰς γυναῖκας καὶ τοὺς δούλους, εὑρήσεις σεαυτὸν δυοκαίδεκα μυριάδων ἀνθρώπων οὐκ ἀρνούμενον εἶναι πλουσιώτερον, ἀλλὰ καὶ τούτους βουλόμενον ὑπερβαλέσθαι. . . κτλ (Kühn edition p. 49).

LL.203–209: these lines recommend that the *astynomoi* in office make a list of all cisterns belonging to private houses in Pergamon and pass it on to the *strategoi*. As the participle καθεσταμένοι allows us to understand, this was a yearly duty that had to be completed by the month *Pantheios*.[203] The text continues by listing technical matters and stresses that during this inspection the *astynomoi* had to make sure that cisterns were *stegnas* and not filled with earth. The subsequent lines restate the same provision, which leads to the question of the meaning of this insistence. In other words, whether it means that cisterns were generally in a poor state or that this emphasis was only meant to put a stop to a process of likely deterioration. This we cannot decide, however we can say with certainty that local authorities were trying to control the number and condition of the water sources with this yearly check.

L. 207 establishes that cisterns had to be στεγνάς: this adjective returns three times within the next 30 lines and only their comprehensive treatment can help determine its exact meaning. The necessary premiss is that it can mean several things, among which 'covered' and 'waterproof.'[204] Archeological data reveals that in Pergamon cisterns were sealed with different types of covers made of stone, but also that they were waterproof.[205] In the text, the adjective *stegnos* appears first in L. 207, then again in LL. 222–223, where it agrees with φρέατα, and finally in L. 236. A new topic is treated in this last case, namely latrines, and the adjective qualifies a *hyponomos*. LL. 222–223 are the most useful to understand the meaning of *stegnos*. These state that cisterns that are

---

[203] Pergamon's calendar is not very well-known, see TRÜMPY 1997, pp. 241–243. In the 2nd century B. C. the Aeolian calendar was still in use in Pergamon and *Pantheios* was one of its months. The time of the year in which it fell, however, is uncertain. Kolbe and Dittenberger tried to place it at the end of Fall or beginning of Winter. According to KOLBE 1902, p. 75: "(Es ist nämlich wahrscheinlich, dass die Astynomen sich zugleich ein Urteil über den Zustand der Zisternen bilden sollten). Das war aber nur möglich, wenn das Wasserstand ein niedriger war, d.h. im Anfanges des Winters". Kolbe assumes also that, since the Aeolian calendar started with the Fall equinox, *Pantheios* must have been the second or the third month in the local calendar. This would have given the offenders the 8 months cited in LL. 212–217, *infra*, within a calendar year to repair their cisterns before a new inspection was carried by the same officials, if their office lasted a year.

[204] KLAFFENBACH 1954, p. 18 discusses the adjective by opposing Kolbe's original view, which supported the meaning "covered", and says: "nun ist aber στεγνός dicht."

[205] See GARBRECHT 2001, pp. 25–27.

not *stegna* could cause damage to neighbors. In this regard, Klaffenbach's comment: "Zisternen, die wasserdurchlässig sind, bilden in der Tat eine Gefahr für die Nachbarn" affirms the reasonableness of this fear. The third column has already given the opportunity to discuss the so-called living quarter of Pergamon, which appears to have been densely built and inhabited. If the majority of these houses had cisterns, it is easy to imagine that those that were not properly maintained or waterproof could cause major damage to neighboring buildings by the leakage of water and then humidity. It is logical to conclude that in LL. 222–223 the adjective must mean "waterproof." Its last instance in the text only reinforces this interpretation as it probably refers to conduits that transported water to/from latrines and, one hopes they did not leak.[206]

If that is the meaning of *stegnos*, the law ordered Pergamon's residents to make sure that the waterproof mortar coat of their cisterns was as effective as possible, lest it damage other neighboring houses. Cisterns, however, were decked too, as further protection, probably so as the water they stored would not be polluted by external elements and also to prevent accidents. This point prompts me to suggest that the first appearance of *stegnos* was conveniently ambiguous.

LL.209–212: these lines list routine provisions and procedures for residents whose cisterns did not pass the inspection. The *astynomoi* had to force the negligent owners to clean their cisterns and, after fining them 100 drachmas for each unattended structure, had to collect the money. The amount is striking: in the Astynomoi law no other misdeed costs residents so much, indeed many of the other attested monetary fines amount to only 5 or 20 drachmas, although sometimes to those one would have to add restoration costs and possibly *hemiolion*. Yet a 100 drachma fine only is very high and comparable only to those that magistrates paid, which, however, were notoriously higher than those for citizens. In this law, for example, the *astynomoi* are liable to this sum twice.[207] Even so, the fine is also markedly higher than the ones magistrates routinely incurred or than the 50 drachmas residents had to pay if they misused

206 *υ* ἀφεδρώνων *υ* οἱ ἀστυνόμοι ἐπιμέ/λειαν ποιείσθωσαν τῶν τε δημοσίων ἀφε/δρ[ώνω]ων καὶ τῶν ἐξ αὐτῶν ὑπονόμων καί, / [ὅσοι ἂν μὴ] στεγνοὶ ὑπάρχωσιν καὶ τῶν - - - /. . . . .

207 See the commentary on LL. 230–232.

public water from fountains. This severity can be only explained with the gravity of the deed. The fine must have been proportional to the importance that water and its infrastructures had in the town. Moreover, their maintenance must have been expensive for the public administration also: LL. 221–222 state that the collected money was reinvested in the cleaning of other, most likely public, cisterns and this was probably another reason for such high fines, *i. e.* to cover high costs.

LL.212–217: record an exception to the rule of LL. 209–212. If a cistern had been filled with earth πρότερον, *i. e.* from before, and was not functioning, the *astynomoi* had to notify the owners. These had 8 months to clean them and, if they had not done so by then, they would be liable to the same fine and be forced to clean them.[208]

Why these cisterns were filled with earth, if they were so vital to the local water distribution system, we can only guess. A plausible hypothesis is that the new aqueducts serving the city had replaced cisterns little by little so that owners left them unattended.[209] Yet emergencies such as wars or even sieges could interfere with aqueducts, and in such situations cisterns would be again crucial to the city's survival. With this regulation the city tried to keep its alternative (?) water supply system in good shape. This must have been a compelling argument in the 2nd century B. C. when the Attalid kingdom and its main urban center were susceptible to sieges. Eumenes II and his successors up to the last member of the dynasty, Attalos III who bequeathed his kingdom to Rome in 133 B. C., participated actively to the affairs of Asia Minor. If and when events escalated in armed conflicts, the city could be exposed to concrete risks. Sources tell of numerous wars in which the last Attalids took part: the continuous fights against the restless Galatians, to Prusias of Bithynia or Pharnakes of Pontos just to name a few.[210] These were real threats against which the local authorities had to take precautions:

[208] For further commentary see Saba 2009, pp. 149–162 where I ask why this exception was made. I hypothesized that the owners had to be tracked down because they rented their property and perhaps were not aware of the cisterns'condition. Nevertheless, they were responsible for their repair.

[209] See Garbrecht 2001, p. 23.

[210] See Gruen 1984, pp. 550–563 and others; Allen 1983, esp. pp. 1–8 and 76–121; Hopp 1977, pp. 34–58; Hansen 1971^2, pp. 66–122; Magie 1950, esp. ch. 1 on the Attalids.

in a siege the first move of the attacking army would be to cut possible acqueduct lines. Under such circumstances then, only water storage units within the city could to help to resist an enemy and thus offer a chance of survival.

LL.217–221: The regulation prescribes that after the fine revenues had been handed over to the treasurers, they be used to cover the restoration costs of cisterns. The inscription does not specify whose cisterns were to be attended to with this money, but I assume that authorities referred to public cisterns. The other option, *i. e.* private cisterns, would be at variance with the statement ordering that negligent owners cleaned and repaired their own property at their own expenses after paying the fine.

Plenty of public property could benefit from this money. For example, public baths had cisterns, which needed regular maintenance. Similar infrastructures can be also found in the so-called fountain houses. These were water deposits that were often located on the way to a sacred precinct, but what is important here is that they were public property.[211] Perhaps the implication was so obvious then that it was thought unnecessary to add details on the legal status of the structures benefiting from these monies.

Finally, the term κατασκευή, which I translate as "repair," deserves a note. Klaffenbach commented on it and said that in this passage it was used instead of ἐπισκευή as this section is concerned only with repairs and does not establish the construction of new structures. Also, he assumed that these repairs were limited to the coating of cisterns.[212] It is, however, possible that it actually referred to a wider range of other routine interventions, which were too well known to be listed. Also, I would not exclude the possibility that the city planned on building new cisterns or water deposits, whether that actually happened or not is a different issue.

LL.221–223: these lines record again the adjective στεγνός.[213] The text asserts that if damages occurred to neighbors because cisterns were not properly coated, their owner would have to pay a fine. In a densely

---

211 See Wulf, 1999, pp. 71–117 for a discussion; see also Saba 2009, pp. 149–162.
212 See Klaffenbach 1954, pp. 18–19.
213 See *supra* the comment to LL. 212–217.

built area, houses could be damaged by water infiltrations coming from poorly maintained cisterns. This seems to overrule the meaning of "covered" for στεγνός, even if uncovered cisterns were also a concern, but not in regard to the danger of structural damage. Rather it was personal safety and water quality that was at risk. For these reasons heavy covers decked cisterns, but the difficulty of lifting them might have discouraged owners from cleaning cisterns regularly, as the repetition of the provision on keeping them clean strongly suggests.[214]

LL.223–227: These lines repeat that the *astynomoi* had to force offenders to repair uncoated cisterns. The parenthetic protasis ἐάν τινες διὰ ταῦτα γείνωνται καταδίκ[αι (LL. 224–225) has created interpretative difficulties in the past. Several scholars thought this implied court activity on the basis of Legras' restoration that had turned καταδίκ[.. into an adjective, *i.e.* καταδίκ[οι. Klaffenbach commented thus: "Die Ergänzung (...) berücksichtigt nicht die Formulierung des Nachsatzes, die die Ergänzung eines Akkusativobjektes zu ἀποδότωσαν aus dem Vorhergehenden verlangt."[215] For this reason he restored the word as *katadikai*, which means in fact only "fine." This allows one to establish that the document prescribes that the *astynomoi* fine the offenders and collect the money, if they thought it appropriate.[216] The necessity of a monetary punishment, along with its exact amount, was left to the *astynomoi*: if a fine was necessary, the injured party would receive reparation. If the officials decided that no damage had occurred, or was neglegible, they would not impose any punishment on the "innocent culprit."

LL.227–230:[217] the closing lines of the paragraph record standard measures against negligent *astynomoi*, but a note is still due because of their formulation. Instead of using the generic formula prescribing that these shall be punished, the text dwells on a very specific task: ὅσοι δ' ἂν

214 See also BRINKER 1986, p. 12.

215 KLAFFENBACH 1954, p. 19.

216 See SCHULTHESS, *RE* X.2 col. 2456/7 where the author quotes the Astynomoi law and says: "Auch in der Astynomen-Ordnung von Pergamon, Dittenberger Or. Gr. 483.212 καὶ ἐάν τινες διὰ ταῦτα γείνωνται καταδίκαι, πράξαντες οἱ ἀστυνόμοι ἀποδότωσαν τοῖς βλαπτομένοις hat, wie πράξαντες beweist, κ(αταδίκαι) klärlich die Bedeutung Buße, Geldstrafe, nicht Verurteilung."

217 I did not respect the syntax of these lines to facilitate the reading of my arguments.

τῶν ἀστυνόμων μὴ / θῶνται τὴν ἐφ' ἑαυτῶν γραφὴν τῶν φρε/άτων εἰς τὸ ἀρχεῖον ἢ μὴ ποιήσωσιν, καθ' ἃ / ὁ νόμος προστάσσει κτλ. The focus is on the yearly list of cisterns and this becomes even more evident when we compare these lines with the most usual and simple formula (for example LL. 14–16): ἐὰν δὲ μὴ ποιήσωσιν / οἱ ἀστυνόμοι, καθάπερ ὁ νόμος προστάσ/σει. The difference lies without doubt in the object to which the officials' misconduct applies: the crucial nature of water resources made them a very high priority for the city and this determined the severity of the punishment.

The often cited list had to be drawn up each year, as the participle καθεσταμένοι suggests, and then submitted to the local archive. Actually, the reference is not properly to an archive, but to the building, the *archeion*, which was the edifice where the *strategoi* operated.[218] The *astynomoi* had to submit the list to the attention of these same magistrates, L. 206, which means that the law prescribed that they deliver this document directly to the *strategoi*'s office. Whether the document was to be updated only, or replaced with a new copy every year is impossible to determine.

LL.230–232: This section contains routine information on who was supposed to collect the money from negligent *astynomoi*. The amount to be gathered is worthy of note and so are the magistrates in charge of the task, namely the *nomophylakes*.

This is their second appearance in the inscription[219] and they collect the substantial amount of 100 drachmas. I have already stressed that this is an unusually high sum, even for negligent officials, and is attested only twice in the whole text. The first time, in L. 20, the *astynomoi* had to pay it on top of the difference of the restoration costs they wrongly estimated (?) and its second appearance is in these lines.

The data on Pergamon's *nomophylakes* are too scanty to allow one to determine their exact role in the public administration. The Astynomoy law shows that they always collected fine-money from the *astynomoi* who did not act according to the law, καθ' ἃ ὁ νόμος προστάσσει. This reference must have been to a very specific, lost law. The *nomophylakes*

218 Parallels for *archeia* in HOLLEAUX, 1942 p. 246

219 The first attestation is in LL. 21–22, see also n. 54 on these magistrates.

might indeed have acted as guardians of the law especially when other officials were involved.

L.233: The text breaks off already in L. 236, but provides the title of a last entry with a genitive, ἀφεδρώνων, that means "latrines."[220] Unfortunately, the content of the specific provisions that were listed on stone is lost and the little that survives is fragmentary. A note on this term is due given its rarity,[221] namely it appears only in the New Testament and later Christian authors, while Classical sources do not record any instance of it. The Suda glosses the term as follows: ὁ δ' ἀφεδρὼν καὶ λυτρώνων βάρβαρα,[222] which confirms its uncommonness.

LL.233–236: Despite the fragmentary state of these last lines, we can gather that the *astynomoi* were responsible for public latrines, or more specifically for the conduits that brought water to clean them. In this section conduits are called *hyponomoi*. These are already attested in the IV column and in one instance they indicate pipes of unknown use and later they are the conduits that serviced fountains. The *hyponomoi* of LL. 233–236 instead must have channeled the outflow of the water from the latrines, since the text specifies that those came ἐξ αὐτῶν.[223]

Latrines of imperial date, but none of Hellenistic period, have been found during the Pergamon excavation.[224] The best-preserved ones belong to public buildings, for example the latrines found by gymnasia or sanctuaries, and have an open access.[225] These are usually bigger rooms

220 On this see again SABA 2011, pp. 24–29.

221 According to Dittenberger, this is a *vox rara OGIS* 483, n. 79. See also STEPHANUS II A, 2621 *s.v.* ἀφεδρών.

222 "while the terms *aphedron* and *lytron* are not proper Greek."

223 See also RADT 1995, p. 204.

224 See RADT 1999(a), pp. 165–166. Also *AvP* VI, p. 91; *AvP* I. 2, for private latrines see for example PINKWART and STAMMNITZ *AvP* XIV, pp. 35–36 with a detailed description of the cleaning system of House III.

225 This was standard practice see NEUDECKER 1994, esp. pp. 14–21. On p. 72 he states: "Latrinen stehen fast nie solitär, sondern bilden zumeinst einen Teil eines größeren Baukomplex mit spezifizierten Aufgaben." His work is quite comprehensive, specifically on Pergamon see p. 139 where he establishes a connection between political importance and the construction of what he calls *Prachtlatrinen*.
More recently, the example of Delos has been discussed in TRÜMPER 2008, esp. pp. 275–278 who refers also to a forthcoming handbook on ancient latrines. In a brief article ZUCHTRIGEL 2008, pp. 85–87 has analysed this passage of the

with several toilet seats placed in a row on an L-shaped bank of stone. Also, the few seats that have survived are made of marble and underneath these run channels in which the water coming from the *peristaseis* flowed. Finally, the water went through a cleaning cycle before going back onto the street. The use of the water from ditches possibly implies that toilets were cleaned mainly when it rained, since it was then that a larger quantity of water was available. In private houses not many latrines are preserved, but the few that are still attested have multiple seats and similar cleaning systems.

L.236: This line has been restored tentatively in several different ways. I retain Klaffenbach's *exempli gratia*.[226] One of the two words out of lacuna is the adjective στεγνός,[227] which I take again to mean 'waterproof' as it qualifies the *hyponomoi* serving latrines.[228] In light of the archaeological material, I assume that the incoming water was channeled through open conduits and only the outflow was carried away through pipes. The text specifies that οἱ ἀστυνόμοι ἐπιμέλειαν ποιείσθωσαν τῶν τε δημοσίων ἀφεδρ[ών]ων καὶ τῶν ἐξ αὐτῶν ὑπονόμων, or in other words they had to check on conduits that brought the water out, which must have meant not only the actual outflow but also the cleaning cycle that the water had to undergo. The water coming from latrines must have been dirty and malodorous: these *hyponomoi* had to be closed cylindrical pipes. The adjective *stegnos* as 'waterproof' is definitely well suited.

Astynomoi law to note again the rarity of the term *aphedron*. According to him, along with the fact that, archaeologically, public latrines are attested only starting from the imperial times, this word could lead one to think that this paragraph had been inserted into the law at a later time. In a rather roundabout way, however, he still concludes that that was not the case. In any case, it is well to remember that "rare" does not mean "non-existent" and that the fact that we have not found Hellenistic public latrines in areas that had been inhabited continuously does not mean that they did not exist.

226 Dittenberger suggested: [ἐάν τινες μὴ σ], but Klaffenbach changed it to [ὅσοι ἂν μὴ] στεγνοὶ ὑπάρχωσιν καὶ τῶν [...]. The reason for rejecting Dittenberger's restoration was its length, although the difference between these two proposals is of two letters only (the Σ of the word στεγνός, which Klaffenbach marks as legible, cannot count as a restored letter). This is far from being a strong argument as on several occasions the mason squeezed letters together, especially ι(s).

227 See *supra* the comment on LL. 203–209.

228 Other possible and attested meanings would be "covered" and "clogged" on which see also the discussion by KLAFFENBACH 1954, p. 19.

5 The *Astynomoi*

These are the last lines of the law that the 2nd century A. D. stone preserves in epigraphic form. The Attalid *prostagma* is the most complete city regulation that has survived and with its many details contribute to an understanding of the daily routine of administering and maintaining a city. It would be more accurate to say that the Astynomoi law is the only surviving regulation we have, which accounts for the paucity of parallels and comparanda to this text. Provisions on "pragmatic" aspects of the life of a *polis* such as building policy, water distribution and the maintainance of its infrastructures, even sanitary ones, do not leave any room for historical reflections or the history of great ideas. This is instead a good example of a pragmatic regulation that lends itself to an interdisciplinary approach by using the available archaeological data, which is fortunately plentiful for Pergamon. The picture we draw is certainly not complete, because the provisions listed are informed by the necessity to regulate the duties of the *astynomoi* who had a very well defined and limited set of duties. Still there is no comparable document to the Astynomoi law when it comes to the description of the mechanisms that allowed a city to work. An office like that of *astynomia* must have existed in every community and *astynomoi* are indeed attested throughout the Mediterranean. In the introduction I pointed out that Athens had them too, but regrettably modern scholarship has used them as model for all other *astynomoi*. In order to ascertain the accuracy, or lack thereof, of this practice I have collected and analyzed all available evidence for these magistrates city by city and compared it with Athens and also Pergamon whenever possible. The officials from the Attalid city, however, still deserve a final, general note.

5.1 The *Astynomoi* in Pergamon

Who were the *astynomoi* in Pergamon? These magistrates do not appear in any other inscription from this town, despite the fact that this regulation suggests that they had a key role in city administration. They constituted a board of magistrates who alternated routine duties with more important tasks, such as controlling water deposits. Their main responsibility pertained to the supervision of buildings and several other city infrastructures, so that they may be, even if loosely, thought of as city inspectors. For example, in the first column the law contains provisions directed to limiting the damages of overbuilding and the illegal constructions in public areas, which they had to see restored. The *astynomoi* were responsible for this and part of their task consisted in fining negligent residents. They did not patrol the city, but relied on conscientious or overzealous residents, as the right of *epilepsis* in L. 197 may show, on the complaints of neighbors, and on magistrates lower in the hierarchy, such as the *amphodarchai*, to direct their attention to infractions and misdeeds.

Their autonomy and authorithy was limited and strictly regulated. For example, only twice are they allowed to determine the amount of fines on the basis of the gravity of the situation: the first time they had to decide whether there was even an infraction in the matter of common walls. Unfortunately, the second instance appears in a very fragmentary context that does not allow one to understand the circumstances.

Their most important duty must have been the supervision of water infrastructures. The text says explicitly that they were in charge of fountains, as well as inspecting cisterns, and also had to make sure that conduits were properly built and functioning. Their duty to check on latrines can be referred back to their water related competences, since they had to survey the functionality of the conduits that served bathroom facilities. The administration of water systems and resources required specific knowledge and skills to the point that even democratic Athens elected those in charge of it instead of drawing them by lot. It is possible that the *astynomoi* were chosen *ad hominem* in Pergamon and had to present credentials to have this office.

Another question pertains to money, as they do not seem to have handled any. They appear as intermediaries that received revenues of exacted fines, which they had to pass on to other officials immediately. If in need of financial support, they had to turn to the *strategoi*, who were ultimately in charge of fining negligent *astynomoi* and if need arose of temporarily taking up their duties. Judicial responsibilities are hinted at in the text too, but there is no strong confirmation of this assumption.

We do not know how many *astynomoi* were active in Pergamon every year, but we are aware that the office had a long life, if the prescript crowning the text of the regulation is, as I believe, a 2nd century A. D. addition. The evidence suggests that this was an important office: their direct supervisors were the *strategoi* who ranked very high-up in the local hierarchy, being top-officials who possibly had to answer only to the ἐπὶ τῆς πόλεως. The inscription also shows that the *astynomoi* directly supervised the *amphodarchai* who were in charge of the matters concerning the territorial units called *amphoda*. More cannot be said, but this suffices to prove that the *astynomoi* had a significant position within the city-administration. They rose above all duties related to living quarters to assume wider responsibilities, which made them the direct persons to approach for citizens but also the link between these and top magistrates.

5.2 The *astynomoi* in the Greek World

Although the Astynomoi law offers a privileged observation point for the activity of *astynomoi*, these are attested in literary and epigraphical sources coming from other geographical and cultural contexts that are often unrelated to each other.[229] The epigraphic evidence, however, is often limited to honorary inscriptions, which do not specify the tasks the *astynomoi* had or, when they do, not in sufficient detail. Literary sources are more informative, but have their disadvantages too since they are few and often tied to theoretical and abstract contexts, which makes it difficult to determine of how much of the reality they represent. Only a combination of these sources could convey a reasonably clear idea of the role the *astynomoi* had, but this is rarely available. As it was to be expected, it is indeed possible in Athens, and because of the evidence the Athenian *astynomia* has become the template for the office in general. I am reluctant to accept this approach to the material, if only for methodological reasons. It is then for this methodological skepticism that in the next few pages I wish to survey the available evidence, starting with Athens and moving on to all the other cities where *astynomoi* are attested. This will make it possible to ascertain not only the *astynomoi*'s duties in different cities, but also either to confirm or get rid of the unthinkingly adopted "Athenian template" prevalent in modern research in this field.

Finally, this review of the evidence must be considered a logical completion to a commentary of the Astynomoi law for a simple, but important reason: in a work that aims to investigate how an office helped to

[229] See also Klingenberg 1983, pp. 227–229.

shape the everyday life of a *polis,* we cannot confine ourselves to *one* test case from which we draw general conclusions, or else we should have been content with an analysis of the Athenian evidence. Each *polis* was an independent entity with its own set of administrative and legal rules. Certainly, a common, underlying pattern may emerge, but we cannot take one model and assume it applies to all other cities.

5.2.1 The Athenian *Astynomoi*

Epigraphic and literary sources give a full rounded picture of the duties and standing of the Athenian *astynomoi*. Recently, Ch. Cox has analyzed and synthesized these sources in an article, which, by stressing the importance of long known but sometimes-neglected evidence, emphasizes the occasional involvement of these officials in property issues, wills, setting and preservation of boundaries.[230] Nevertheless a brief review of the Athenian evidence is due.

The literary *locus classicus* for Athenian *astynomia* is *Ath. Pol.* 50.2:[231]

. . . καὶ ἀστυνόμοι δέκα. τούτων δὲ ε′ μὲν ἄρχουσιν ἐν Πειραιεῖ, πέντε δ' ἐν ἄστει, καὶ τάς τε αὐλητρίδας καὶ τὰς ψαλτρίας καὶ τὰς κιθαριστρίας οὗτοι σκοποῦσιν ὅπως μὴ πλείονος ἢ δυεῖν δραχμαῖν μισθωθήσονται, κἂν πλείους τὴν αὐτὴν σπουδάσωσι λαβεῖν, οὗτοι διακληροῦσι καὶ τῷ λαχόντι μισθοῦσιν. καὶ ὅπως τῶν κοπρολόγων[232] μηδεὶς ἐντὸς ι′ σταδίων τοῦ τείχους καταβαλεῖ κόπρον ἐπιμελοῦνται, καὶ τὰς ὁδοὺς κωλύουσι κατοικοδομεῖν, καὶ δρυφάκτους ὑπὲρ τῶν ὁδῶν ὑπερτείνειν, καὶ ὀχετοὺς μετεώρους εἰς τὴν ὁδὸν

[230] Cox, 2007, pp. 769–775.

[231] See Cox, 2007, pp. 769–775 and Rhodes 1981, pp. 573–575. Past scholarship assumed that this passage described the duties of the *astynomoi* in Athens and everywhere else in the Greek world exhaustively.

[232] The *koprologoi* were scavengers. They rarely appear in the surviving sources. Predictably, Aristophanes mentions them a few times for example in *Pax*, l. 9; *Vespae*, l. 1184, while in the *Ath. Pol.* they appear only this once. I doubt if they were public slaves or officials, see Owens 1983, pp. 48–50, as it was thought earlier. This latter misunderstanding was generated by a passage in [Demosth.] *Contra Aristog.* XX. 49. 7, on which Vatin 1976, p. 558: "le texte de Démosthène montre bien qu'il s'agit de personages très modestes et il ne faut probablement pas le confondre avec les astynomes mentionnés par Aristote, lesquel avaient d'ailleurs d'autres functions. Il est donc probable que les κοπρώνων ἐπιστάτας sont précisément les *coprologues* deja connus." There was no *arche* called *koprologia*. The collection of garbage was supervised by other officials, such as the *astynomoi*, but carried out by hired personnel, namely the *koprologoi*. See also *supra* the commentary to LL. 90–93.

ἔκρουν ἔχοντας ποιεῖν, καὶ τὰς θυρίδας εἰς τὴν ὁδὸν ἀνοίγειν. καὶ τοὺς ἐν ταῖς ὁδοῖς ἀπογιγνομένους ἀναιροῦσιν, ἔχοντες δημοσίους ὑπηρέτας.[233]

This passage states that Athens had ten *astynomoi*, five of whom were active in the Peiraeus and five in the city. Their duties were wide-ranging as they controlled the compensation given to entertainers and oversaw the cleaniless and general conditions of streets.[234] Further literary testimonies for the Athenian *astynomoi* are in Plato's *Laws* as well as in the Aristotle's *Politics*. These largely confirm the data provided by the *Athenaion Politeia*, but also add a few details. For example, Aristotle, *Politics* 1321b states:

ἑτέρα δὲ ἐπιμέλεια ταύτης ἐχομένη καὶ σύνεγγυς ἡ τῶν περὶ τὸ ἄστυ δημοσίων καὶ ἰδίων, ὅπως εὐκοσμία ᾖ, καὶ τῶν πιπτόντων οἰκοδομημάτων καὶ ὁδῶν σωτηρία καὶ διόρθωσις, καὶ τῶν ὁρίων τῶν πρὸς ἀλλήλους, ὅπως ἀνεγκλήτως ἔχωσιν, καὶ ὅσα τούτοις ἄλλα τῆς ἐπιμελείας ὁμοιότροπα. καλοῦσι δ' ἀστυνομίαν οἱ πλεῖστοι τὴν τοιαύτην ἀρχήν, ἔχει δὲ μόρια πλείω τὸν ἀριθμὸν, ὧν ἑτέρους ἐφ' ἕτερα καθιστᾶσιν ἐν ταῖς πολυανθρωποτέραις πόλεσιν, οἷον τειχοποιοὺς καὶ κρηνῶν ἐπιμελητὰς καὶ λιμένων φύλακας.[235]

---

233 "(they choose by lot κληροῦνται) ten *astynomoi*, of them five discharge their duties in the Piraeus, five in the city. They are in charge of controlling flute-girls, harp-players and lyre-girls, so that they are not hired for more than two drachmas, and in case several men fight over the same girl, the *astynomoi* should cast lots to decide who is going to hire her. They shall also care that none of the *koprologoi* throw dung within 10 stadia from town. Also they should stop people from building on the streets and balconies from protruding onto the street, and that surfacing channels have a direct outflow on the streets and that windows open on the streets. Finally, they collect the bodies of those who passed away on the street, but they have public slaves for this task."

234 See Cox 2007, p. 773 for the fights among men who wanted to hire the same women. Apparently, these turned into physical confrontations often and required the authorities' attention. One point of Cox's reading is not completely accurate. On p. 770 she comments on the *Ath. Pol.* thus: "They also would not allow gutters discharging water into the street to be built overhead . . ." where "overhead" is the translation of μετεώρους on which see my commentary *supra*. She must be following Rhodes 1981, p. 575 where the same inaccuracy occurs.

235 "Another curatorship very close to this takes care of the public and private matters in the city, so that everything is well-managed, the safety and rectification of falling buildings and of streets, and boundaries between properties, so that there will not be conflicts, and all the tasks similar to these. The majority calls this magistracy *astynomia*; it has a rather large number of departments, of which the various positions are filled by various (officials) in populous cities, for example *teichopoioi*, curators of fountains and harbor guards."

The philosopher sketches the duties of a generic board of *astynomoi*. Still, it is hard to resist the temptation to compare them with the Athenian officials. The first lines of this passage do not add anything new, but of some interest is their task to check the boundaries between properties and whether dwellers made proper use of them. Moreover, in the last sentence, Aristotle specifies that in populous cities the office of *astynomia* had sub-sections and specific duties were taken over by officials with other titles. Among them the κρηνῶν ἐπιμελητής stands out, whose duties, namely the supervision of fountains and water, were assigned to the *astynomoi* (IV col.) in Pergamon.

Plato's *Laws* describes *astynomoi* in the section following the theoretical framework on which rest the political institutions of his ideal *polis*.[236] He asserts the necessity of appointing magistrates in charge of roads, buildings and the like and also sets up a theoretical triad of officials consisting of *agoranomoi*, *astynomoi* and sacred magistrates. The *astynomoi*'s duties are described in greater detail in *Leges* 763c–e:[237]

τὸ δὲ μετὰ τοῦτο ἀρχόντων αἱρέσεως ἀγορανόμων πέρι καὶ ἀστυνόμων πέρι ἦν ἡμῖν ἑπόμενον. ἕποιντο δ' ἂν ἀγρονόμοις γε ἀστυνόμοι τρεῖς ἑξήκοντα οὖσιν, τριχῇ δώδεκα μέρη τῆς πόλεως διαλαβόντες, μιμούμενοι ἐκείνους τῶν τε ὁδῶν ἐπιμελούμενοι τῶν κατὰ τὸ ἄστυ καὶ τῶν ἐκ τῆς χώρας λεωφόρων εἰς τὴν πόλιν ἀεὶ τεταμένων καὶ τῶν οἰκοδομιῶν, ἵνα κατὰ νόμους γίγνωνται πᾶσαι, καὶ δὴ καὶ τῶν ὑδάτων, ὁπόσ' ἂν αὐτοῖς πέμπωσι καὶ παραδιδῶσιν οἱ φρουροῦντες τεθεραπευμένα, ὅπως εἰς τὰς κρήνας ἱκανὰ καὶ καθαρὰ πορευόμενα, κοσμῇ τε ἅμα καὶ ὠφελῇ τὴν πόλιν. δεῖ δὴ καὶ τούτους δυνατούς τε εἶναι καὶ σχολάζοντας τῶν κοινῶν ἐπιμελεῖσθαι· διὸ προβαλλέσθω μὲν πᾶς ἀνὴρ ἐκ τῶν μεγίστων τιμημάτων ἀστυνόμον ὅν ἂν βούληται διαχειροτονηθέντων δὲ καὶ ἀφικομένων εἰς ἓξ οἷς ἂν πλεῖσται γίγνωνται, τοὺς τρεῖς ἀποκληρωσάντων οἷς τούτων ἐπιμελές, δοκιμασθέντες δὲ ἀρχόντων κατὰ τοὺς τεθέντας αὐτοῖς νόμους.[238]

---

[236] On these magistrates see Piérart 2008^2, pp. 291–310; Morrow 1960, pp. 181–183.

[237] The *astynomoi* appear throughout Plato's work; see 759 a; d; 779 c; 845 e. and others.

[238] "After these magistracies, there follows the choice of *agoranomoi* and *astynomoi*; three *astynomoi* come after the *agronomoi* who are sixty, dividing the twelve parts of the city in three sections, copying them (the *agronomoi*), since they see to the streets crossing town and the *leophoroi* that go from the countryside to the town and the buildings, so that they all conform to the laws. Also, they

Plato lists tasks that strongly resemble those of the Athenian *astynomoi*, the only, although major, difference being the method of appointment. In contrast with real Athens, in Plato's Magnesia these magistrates were elected among the wealthiest members of the citizen body, as the property requirement shows. After six candidates had been chosen, the lot was used to select the final three men.[239] Plato also records judicial powers for *astynomoi*, as they judge cases, punish and fine offenders in several circumstances.[240]

To these sources that are in a way abstract and only partly refer to the real Athens, Cox has added testimonies from the orators where the *astynomoi* appear sporadically to regulate matters concerning private property.[241] The epigraphic data completes the literary evidence; after all, as Hennig has reminded us, the city magistrates were the source of inspiration for the ideal ones, not the other way around.[242]

If the literary *locus classicus* for Athenian *astynomia* is the *Ath. Pol.*, the review of the epigraphic evidence must start with *IG* II^2 380, commonly known as the Agoranomic law, although I prefer to retain the *IG*'s description for it, namely *de Agoranomorum officiis.* The Athenians passed this – in fact – decree in 320/19 B. C. to establish anew the duties of the *agoranomoi*[243] in the Peiraeus for the procession for Zeus Soter and Dionysus. Later in the text, these tasks are said to extend τὸν λοιπὸν χρόνον, L. 35,[244] which grants the document a more permanent character than decrees normally have.

---

attend to water, which is passed to them by the guards in a good state, so that it beautifies and supplies the city, coming in sufficient quantity and clean to the fountains. These men ought to be powerful and have enough time to attend to public matters. As a consequence, each man should nominate as *astynomos* the one whom he chooses among the wealthiest; after a vote and after coming down to the six with the most votes, the three who will have the office are selected by lot; after passing scrutiny they shall carry out their duties according to the laws."

239 See *Ath. Pol.* 50; DEMOSTH. *In Timocr.* 24. 112 testify that *astynomoi* in Athens were chosen by lot; PIÉRART 2008^2, pp. 294–295; MORROW 1960, p. 185.

240 See PL. *Leg.* 764c; 779c; 844c; 845c.

241 I refer to COX 2007 for details that it would be pointless to repeat here.

242 See HENNIG 1995, pp. 235–236.

243 On these magistrates see STANLEY 1976. On the historical context PODDIGHE 2002, esp. pp. 41–45, who however overinterprets the role of the *astynomoi* and the meaning of *IG* II^2 380.

244 In *IG* this is line 34, but OLIVER 2003, p. 49, n. 32 asserts that a new first line can be seen on the stone with the invocation ϑεοί. LIDDEL 2003, p. 81, n. 18 confirms this after consulting the squeeze in Princeton.

Agoranomoi and *astynomoi* sometimes appear together, but in *IG* II^2 380 this association has a different meaning since supposedly by passing it the authorities intended to eliminate *astynomia* and assign its duties to the *agoranomoi*.[245] This interpretation of the document, however, is subject to debate and not everybody agrees that its ultimate consequence was the disappearance of the board of the *astynomoi*. To start with, the text confines its authority to Peiraeus where, as the *Ath. Pol.* says, five *astynomoi* operated, the others five being in the city. Furthermore, it lists only a limited number of duties overwhelmingly related to the procession for Zeus Soter and Dionysos. Still, it is undeniable that the aims of the document, along with its wording, are ambiguous. Perhaps only the few tasks the text lists here were to be removed from the care of the *astynomoi*, which would eliminate the almost disturbing hypothesis that this office was abolished completely.[246] But even if that was the aim, it must have been limited to Peiraeus. Be that as it may, *IG* II^2 380 remains an important document to determine the role of the *astynomoi* in Athens. Apart from processions, the last few lines provide a more general overview of their tasks, which were not only related to cultic activity as several other surviving inscriptions led to believe in the past. It was because of those that Klingenberg defined the *astynomoi* "Fest-sakral Polizei", which stresses their duties within the *polis'* sacred life, but neglects the rest of the evidence on their civic activities.[247]

A last and later document must be accounted for too, namely a dedicatory inscription that Peppas Delmousou has recently discussed anew.[248] The text is inscribed on two fragments that this scholar has joined, *IG* II^2 3939 + 2878, and dated to the age of Augustus on the ba-

---

245 LL. 17–18: ἐπειδὴ δὲ καὶ ἡ τῶν ἀστυνόμων ἐπιμέ/λεια προστέτακται τοῖς ἀγορ[α]νόμοις. Since the tasks of the *astynomoi* were passed onto the *agoranomoi*.

246 So Oliver 2003, p. 49, n. 32. The last few lines, 35 to the end, however, weaken this thesis as more general prescriptions appear, such as the prohibition to litter. *IG* II^2 659 passed in 283/2 B. C. is always cited after 380 because is the next text to mention again the *astynomoi*. This means that even if *astynomia* had really been abolished in 320, it was reinstated at the latest in 282. For the 3rd century see also *IG* II^2 704 honoring the *astynomoi* who took care properly of the celebrations for Asklepios.

247 For the *Fest-sakral Polizei* see Klingenberg 1983, p. 230. Activity of regular, secular officials in sacred events is common, see *supra* especially on the role of the *agoranomos* in Andania, see Harter-Uibopuu 2002, esp. pp. 135–139; and Chandezon 2000, pp. 79–85.

248 Peppas Delmousou 2004, pp. 121–138.

sis of prosopography.[249] The inscription says: [Κρά]της Ἀριστονίκο[υ] / [Φλυεύ]ς καὶ Δημήτριος / [Κι]νέου Κυδαθηναιεύς / [γ]όνωι δὲ Θεμίσωνος Ἀνα/φλυστίου ἀστυ/νομήσαντες / ἀνέθηκαν,[250] and is the only instance in which *astynomoi* appear in the Roman period in Athens.[251] Peppas Delmousou has noted that these two men dedicated – of all things – a *sekoma* to an unknown deity. *Sekomata* were tables with hollow sections of different diameters that must have been used to measure dry and liquid products and have been found in several areas of the Mediterranean. The object on which the text was inscribed has led Peppas Delmousou to ask why *astynomoi* would dedicate such an object and she reached the conclusion that they used it when they were active in their office to determine measurements.[252] According to the *Ath. Pol.* 51, in the 4th century this task was under the care of *agoranomoi* and *metronomoi* and despite the small amount of evidence in our possession it seems unlikely that their duties had passed *en bloc* to the *astynomoi*,[253] especially since at least the *agoranomoi* continued to exist. This is certainly a difficult point, which clearly we cannot resolve, and that Peppas Delmousou has attempted to clarify by considering the Roman influence on Athenian institutions. In other words, she thinks that in this inscription one should explain the *astynomoi* as *praetores urbani*. This translation of the Latin office into Greek is indeed attested in Cassius Dio's work,[254] but he uses it only to describe Roman citizens holding Roman posts, not Greek institutions. Also, I find very hard to believe that the actual Greek *astynomoi* had been assigned duties that were so far off their traditional tasks and which the still existing *agoranomoi* discharged routinely. There is no direct evidence to support the proposal of Peppas Delmousou, which is certainly based on a good observation regarding the votive object, but relies otherwise on very weak foundation. All this dedication reveals is

249 Her detailed discussion is on p. 129.

250 I did not reproduce here the three letters that should represent units of measurement, on which see Peppas Delmousou 2004, esp. pp. 124–127 with further bibliographical references.

251 The text has hardly been discussed, but see Gaegan 1967, pp. 125–126.

252 On these objects see Peppas Delmousou 2004, pp. 122–124; Stroud 1998, pp. 56–61.

253 See again Gaegan 1967, pp. 123–125 who suggests that the *metronomoi* over time had disappeared and their duties passed to the *agoranomoi*.

254 Peppas Delmousou 2004, p. 131 referring to Mason 1974, esp. p. 16; 27; 156 citing Cass. Dio 42, 22, 2; 46, 45, 2.

that *astynomoi* still existed under Augustus but I cannot agree to seeing them as *praetores urbani* in Athens.

Overall, the evidence from the Attic city suggests that its 4th century B. C. *astynomoi* had to oversee streets and buildings, make sure that property limits were respected and also wielded judicial power in a few matters. What is not to be forgotten is that their tasks included the surveillance and care of the secular aspects of religious events. Finally, we can infer that the board of the *astynomoi* was already well established by the 4th century B. C. and survived into Roman times, but also that we are unaware of any change in their duties, if any occurred. Their attested tasks ranged widely, but not as much as those of the *astynomoi* from Pergamon, which was, however, a smaller city.

5.2.2 Cycladic Islands

5.2.2.1 Keos

The island of Keos is located off the coast of Attica to the Southeast. Today a few hours suffice to reach it from the Piraeus, but even in antiquity this could be accomplished in a relatively short time, namely about a day.[255] The island had four cities, Ioulis, Koresia, Karthaia and Poiessa. Only Ioulis was located inland while the other three were coastal towns. This is not the place for reviewing the complex history of the island and the equally intricated relations among its cities, but a brief account is called for before proceding to the analysis of its *astynomoi*. The local epigraphic record mentions them twice for the mid of the 4th century B. C. circa and to these decades I confine my brief historical account.[256] It is necessary to bear in mind that the key to the understanding of Keos is the reciprocal relation of its four *poleis*, which unfortunately is difficult to reconstruct. The sources seem to indicate that they had a history of consorting together, even institutionally, but whenever the island was under the more or less direct control of an external power this "union" was discouraged, for obvious reasons.

255 BRUN 1989, p. 121. WALSER 2009, pp. 145–148 offers a brief overview of the available archaeological results especially in regard to urban settlements.

256 The complex institutional history of Keos in the 3rd and 2nd century is still debated, see recently WALSER 2009, p. 145; REGER 2001, esp. p. 171; IDEM 1988.

Keos had been a member of both Athenian leagues and the foundation document of the second, known also as the decree of Aristoteles, provides direct evidence for the participation of all four cities, although with a *caveat*: Poiessa appears on its own (L. 82), while the other three are listed together under the heading Κείων (LL. 119–122).[257] This peculiar, more autonomous (?) position for Poiessa is attested again in the 4th century, although other epigraphic testimonies allow for the hypothesis that in the 60s a union of all towns was established.[258] One of the two texts attesting to this complete (?) union names *astynomoi*. This is *StV* II² 287 (*IG* XII 5. 594) establishing *isopoliteia* between the Keans and the Euboean city of Histiaea in a year between 364–362 B. C.[259] This dating does not rely on specific internal data, rather on the general historical situation suggesting that the Keans attempted to secede from the alliance with Athens at the time of Thebes' activities under the leadership of Epaminondas. In the treaty the Keans appear as one community and use the adjective Κεῖος for individuals without specifying their poleic provenance. The document is fragmentary and contains typical and less typical elements of isopolity, prominent among which are the clauses that aim to facilitate the temporary permanence of citizens of both communities in the signing partner's territory. It is in this context that *astynomoi* appear (*StV* II² 287,LL. 17–21):

---

[257] *IG* II² 43, now see RHODES and OSBORNE 2003, n. 22.

[258] This "union" has been variously called *sympoliteia*, league, or federation, but the sources do not allow deciding on its exact nature. See BRUN 1989, esp. pp. 128–130 and LEWIS 1962, pp. 1–4. The latter thinks that Poiessa was excluded from this agreement: the treaties that testify to the union refer to*trittyes* and according to Lewis, these are hard to reconcile with a union of 4 cities. The evidence is collected and discussed anew by BRUN 1989, pp. 121–126. The 3rd and 2nd century instead saw the creation of actual *sympoliteiai* with which two cities (Poiessa and Koresia) merged into the other two (Karthaia and Ioulis), see STRAB. X.5.6 = 486–487 C, recent bibliography *supra* n. 257. See NIGDELIS 1990 for a discussion of the settlements and the political relations among the *poleis* of the Cycladic islands, esp. pp. 199–252; pp. 233–234 for *sympoliteia* and the magistrates of the Keian cities.

[259] On this treaty GAUTHIER 1972, pp. 356–357; GAWANTKA 1975 is the only existing work on isopolity, but focuses on the *Rechtsgeschichte* and the evidence is not treated systematically; BRUN 1989, p. 124 and again pp. 133–134. *Isopoliteia* is normally translated as "potential citizenship" and its grant entails a (mainly) bilateral exchange of (potential) citizenship.

(part of an oath) - - - - -ἐπι]-
μέλεσθαι δὲ ἐγ Κέωι [μὲν τήν τε βουλὴν καὶ τοὺς]
[πρ]οβούλους καὶ τ[οὺς . . 12 c. . . καὶ τοὺς]
[ἀσ]τυνόμους τῶ[ν Ἱστιαιέων, ἐν Ἱστιαίαι δὲ τοὺς]
[ἄρχ]ο[ν]τα̣[ς ? - - -

These few lines are the corollary to enrollment clauses prescribing the procedure for an eventual switch of citizenship and to other provisions that eased trading between these communities. After the reference to an oath, the text names the magistrates in charge of caring for the partner community's citizens who made a temporary halt there. Histiaea's responsible magistrates are no longer attested, but those of Keos are still readable and among them figure the *astynomoi*.[260] This does not mean that among their routine duties there was that of controlling visiting foreigners. On the contrary, I must stress the exceptional character of this task of theirs from a diplomatic point of view. The special relation *isopoliteia* had established between Keos and Histiaea made it possible for these Euboean citizens to have direct access to magistrates and institutions that otherwise were off limits to foreigners, namely *astynomoi*. In other words, even if Histiaeans did not switch citizenship, their status and standing in Keos was considerably better than that of any other foreigner.

Astynomoi appear a second time in Keos in an inscription, *StV* II^2 320 (*IG* II^2 1128), that was found on the Athenian Akropolis and is now stored in the Epigraphic Museum of Athens.[261] This records three decrees from Carthaia, Koresia and Ioulis that stipulate the Athenian monopoly on Kean ruddle.[262] The first decree from Carthaia is known only from its last few fragmentary lines, but the other two documents are better preserved. The chronology is not easy to determine, but scholarship usually opts for the mid of the 4th century B. C.[263] Of relevance here is the second decree from Coresia establishing the monopoly of ruddle, the beneficiary of the right to export it and harbor fees. After dealing

260 Gauthier 1972, p. 357.
261 Now see Rhodes and Osborne 2003, n. 40, pp. 204–209.
262 For the historical context see Dreher 1989, pp. 263–270.
263 Brun 1989, p. 123: “post 362.”

with these matters, the text addresses the legal consequences that those who would not respect these provisions had to face. (LL. 16–17):

. . . . · τὴν δὲ ἔνδειξιν εἶν]/αι πρὸς τοὺς ἀστυνόμους, τοὺς δὲ ἀστυνόμους δοῦνα[ι τὴν ψῆφον περὶ αὐτῆς τριάκοντα ἡ]/μερῶν εἰς τὸ δικαστήριον· τῶι δὲ φήναντι ἢ ἐνδείξαντ[ι . . 18 c. . . τῶν ἡμι]/σ[έ]ων· κτλ[264]

If these provisions had not been followed, the *astynomoi* were to be notified and had to cast a vote on the matter and bring it to court within thirty days. This text seems to tie these magistrates with trade, even if indirectly, and turns them into persons to contact for citizens who intended to bring up an accusation for misconduct in the matter. Even if the general context is lost, this clause may still reflect their limited judicial capacity for which there may be a parallel in the III column of Astynomoi law where, however, it is not certain whether these magistrates had to cast a vote directly on the matter of collapsing walls.[265]

The evidence for Keos' *astynomoi* is slim and not unproblematic. To start with, in one inscription they are "magistrates of the Keans," but in the second case they appear to be only the *astynomoi* of Coresia.[266] In both cases, they operated within the institutions as persons to contact for citizens and potential citizens. The testimony of *IG* XII 5, 594 should not be underestimated as it shows that they could have *helped* the Histiaeans who sojourned temporarily on the island: probably, they had this task

264 Transl. Rhodes and Osborne: "Indication (*endeixis*) to be to the *astynomoi* and the *astynomoi* are to give the vote about it in court within thirty days. To the man who makes the exposure (*phasis*) or the indication (*endeixis*) of the halves." On *endeixis* see MacDowell 1991, pp. 187–189 who uses it to define *phasis, i. e.* another procedure by which a case could be initiated. With *endeixis* a denouncer had only to point to the offender, but did not have to show the goods that triggered the accusation. MacDowell defines these procedures for Athens, to which those of Keos could be related, more than having been imposed upon. Also, Rubinstein 2003, pp. 89–90, n. 5 commented on this by stressing that there are "important deviations" in the way the procedures are applied in the two communities, so also Rhodes and Osborne, n. 40 quoted by Rubinstein, pp. 208–209: "it is more likely that Athenian and Kean law shared closely similar procedures than that the Athenians stipulated the procedure to be employed."

265 See *supra* comment to LL. 123–128.

266 Both texts roughly date to the mid of the 4th century B. C. and it is possible that the three cities of Carthaia, Coressa and Ioulis operated as one institutional entity. The *isopoliteia* was stipulated between Histiaia and – in general – with these three cities of Keos and needed not be further regulated, the monopoly of ruddle was a different matter that had more immediate economic repercussions. Possibly this caused the separate decrees of the three otherwise associated cities.

because they were aware of local issues and institutional mechanisms. Each (?) city in Keos possibly had *astynomoi*, whether they were united institutionally or not, in charge of duties that pertained to daily matters within their *polis* and were contact persons for citizens.

5.2.2.2 Tenos

Astynomoi appear in Cycladic Tenos. They are mentioned several times in documents that *IG* describes as *catalogi*, *IG* XII 5. 872; 880–883 that date to different centuries the latest belonging to the 1st century B. C. and the earliest to the 4th and 3rd. Among them, the best-known and most important text is *IG* XII 5. 872 recording the sale of plots of land, houses and the payment of dowries to be registered before the *astynomoi*.[267] This discloses legal competencies for these officials and has led scholars to assume that in Tenos they had more responsibilities than in other areas. Their apparently heavier workload, however, might depend on the size of Tenos, a small island that counted only one *polis*.[268] The observation found in the *Politics* of Aristotle (1321 b) for which bigger cities tended to have more and more specialized magistrates than smaller communities is apt here and reflects the basic principle of the division of labor.

The other surviving Tenian catalogues record lists of magistrates, but are not particularly informative. Even the attempt to establish a hierarchy within magistracies on the basis of the information they give fails. The order of appearance of officials in *IG* XII.5 881–883[269] varies and these texts do not even always mention the same boards; for example, the second list of *IG* XII.5 881 omits the *astynomoi*, which are otherwise attested.

5.2.2.3 Delos

Only five Delian inscriptions testify to the existence of *astynomoi*. Three of these are honorific texts,[270] while the most informative is *IG*

[267] See also *SEG* L, 1687.
[268] See Etienne 1984, pp. 205–208.
[269] Etienne 1990, pp. 145–146.
[270] *IG* XI.4, 1144; 1145 and 1147 are honorific; *IG* IX.4 1296 A and B; Feyel and Prost 1998, pp. 455–459.

XI.4.1296 A and B, that has been dated to the mid of the 3rd century B. C. on paleographical grounds. The document is opisthographic and the two sides are almost exact copies, but for one line.[271] The inscription confirms that in Delos the *astynomoi* constituted a board and that sacred and secular sphere interacted, which, however, is nothing new.[272] Here, I reproduce Face A since it is the most complete:

[τ]άδε ἐπεύχονται ἱερεῖς τε καὶ / ἱ̣έρειαι κατὰ τὰ πάτρια· ὅστις ἐ/γ Δήλου ἀνδράποδον ἐξάγει εἴ/τε ἄκον εἴτε ἑκὸν ἢ ἐκ τῶν τε/μενῶν τῶν ἱερῶν τῶν τοῦ θεοῦ̣ / ἐπὶ βλάβηι τοῦ δεσπότου, ἐξώ/λη εἶναι καὶ αὐτὸν καὶ γένος / καὶ οἴκησιν τὴν ἐκείνου· καὶ ὅστι̣ς / συνειδὼ̣ς μὴ δηλώσει ἐν τοῖς ἀσ̣/τυνόμοις τοῖς αὐτοῖς ἔνοχος ἔσ/τω· καὶ εἴ τίς τι ἄλλο ἐγ Δήλου βιάζ[οι]/το παρὰ τὰ πάτρια τὰ Δηλίων, ἐξώλ[η] / εἶναι αὐτὸν καὶ οἴκησιν τὴν ἐκείνο[υ]. / ἀστυνόμοι ἐπιμελήθησαν Σα̣ρπη/δὼν Καρνέου, Ὀνησιγένης Θέμωνο[ς], / Ἀρίγνωτος.[273]

This text contains *arai*, but of interest here are LL. 8–11 that establish that those who did not report the flight of slaves to the *astynomoi* would be held legally responsible.[274] The first editor commented on the duties of these magistrates as follows: "Ils protégeaient les esclaves et les biens des habitants de l'île contre les pirates, et probablement contre les voleurs locaux. Ils recevaient les dénonciations"[275] and thus wanted to identify the perpetrators with an external enemy. Yet, the inference that the local *astynomoi* were in charge of defending properties of the island against pirates, or that some sort of internal opposition determined the passing of this provision is reading too much into this text and their du-

---

271 *Editio princeps* in VALLOIS 1914, pp. 250–251, more recently GSCHNITZER 1989, pp. 31–33. Vallois hypothesized that the Delian *astynomoi* were three just as in Tenos.

272 VIAL 1985, pp. 236–237.

273 "Priests and priestesses pray a curse according to the ancestral laws. If anybody takes out of Delos a slave whether willing or unwilling or from the precincts of the god thus damaging the owner, he, his clan and his household shall be exiled. If anybody does not report (this) to the *astynomoi*, he shall be liable to the same curse. And if anybody takes away with force anything from Delos against the laws of the Delians, he shall be exiled and his house too. The *astynomoi* in charge are Sarpedon son of Karneas, Onesigenes son of Themon, Arignotos."

274 Data on Delian slavery are scarce see BRUNEAU 1989, p. 41. Ancient sources testify to a revolt in 130 and to the slave market, but no information on slaves' conditions survives. VIAL 1985, p. 149 and BRUNEAU 1989, p. 44 think that this text deals with sacred slaves employed in Rheneia and Mykonos.

275 See VALLOIS 1914, p. 252.

ties. A conservative and more appropriate reading would be that Delian *astynomoi* watched over slaves' attempts to escape and could take legal action against those who did not pass on information as required by law. They had some form of judicial power and clearly acted in the large harbor area of the island. The question as to whether they had competencies directly tied to the local market must remain unanswered.

These same lines appear hardly altered in another, later inscription. It consists of two non-contiguous fragments, which were joined first by Tréheux and now, despite many initial criticisms, are firmly believed to be one document.[276] The inscription dates to the first decades of the 2nd century B. C. (between 180–166 B. C.) and tries to discipline the behavior of pilgrims and slaves in the sanctuary of Apollon (fragment A), while a second fragment (B) prohibits the presence of animals within the *temenos*, establishes the fines for the offenders and lists those responsible for the collection of the money and the entire procedure. The decree ends in line 16 with the mention of a vote. Finally, to all this, the fragmentary B. LL. 17–26 are appended and record *arai* that are formulated just like in *IG* XI.4.1296.[277]

ἐπεύχονται ἱε[ρ]εῖς καὶ ἱέρειαι κατὰ τὰ πά/τρ[ια ὅ]στις ἐγ Δήλου ἀνδράποδα ἐξάγει εἴ/[τε ἄκοντα εἴτ]ε ἑ[κ]όντα ἐκ τῶν τεμενῶν / [τῶν ἱερῶν τῶν τοῦ ϑεοῦ] ἐπὶ βλάβηι τοῦ δεσπό/[του, ἐξώλη εἶναι καὶ αὐτὸ]ν καὶ γένος καὶ οἴ/[κησιν τὴν ἐκείνου]· καὶ εἴ τις συνειδὼς / [μὴ δηλώσειεν ἐν τοῖς ἀστ]υνόμοις, τοῖς αὐτοῖς / [ἔνοχον εἶναι· καὶ εἴ τίς τι ἄλλο βι]άζοιτο / [παρὰ τὰ πάτρια τῶν Δηλίων, ἐξώλη εἶναι αὐτὸ]ν καὶ γένος / [καὶ οἴκησιν τὴν ἐκείνου]

The transcription shows heavy restorations, which, needless to say, were done on the basis of *IG* XI 1296 A and B.[278] This suggests that the *arai* are earlier than the rest of the inscription, to which however the text refers, frag. B, L. 4. They must have been reproduced here for their ritual and legally coercive value,[279] but can tell us very little on institutions. *Astynomoi* must still have existed at the beginning of the

276 See FEYEL and PROST 1998, p. 455; on this see *SEG* XLVIII, 1037 and DUBOIS *BE* 2000, n. 490. A new edition of the text in LUPU 2005, pp. 22–23; CHANDEZON 2003, n. 31 on B, LL. 1–14.

277 I record here the text as in LUPU 2005, p. 23.

278 See FEYEL and PROST 1998, p. 461.

279 See RUBINSTEIN 2007, pp. 269–286 who rejects Ziebarth and Latte's early hypothesis on the trivialization of *arai*'s significance in the Hellenistic age.

2nd century B. C. probably with very similar duties as in the past, but no other conclusion can be drawn.

Two other short texts from Delos deserve mention, *IG* XI.4, 1144 and 1145 dated respectively to the mid 3rd and 2nd century B. C.[280] Both inscriptions record dedications to Hermes and Aphrodite by an *agoranomos* and an *astynomos*. The significance, as far as the interaction between magistracies and cult is concerned, is not easy to grasp,[281] but their pairing up points to a possible collaboration.[282] It is possible that here their joint appearance could indicate that they worked together in the harbor. This is not an unlikely hypothesis, since an intervention of *astynomoi* in commercial areas and activities has left traces in other documents even from the Cyclades, but solid proof is lacking.[283]

The evidence for *astynomoi* in Delos is rather scarce; they had a limited judicial power as their duty to police public and private goods may show. It is difficult to draw a parallel with Athens or Pergamon, but, because of the strong tie Delos had with the former, administrative similarity, especially for the Hellenistic period, cannot be overruled. Still, this is merely a suggestion: the Delian dedications do not tell one anything specific, while the quotation of *astynomoi* in the *arai* prompts an observation or two. *Astynomoi* had a police-role and were the board to which denunciations could or had to be made under certain circumstances. This partially recalls the provisions attested in column IV, LL. 180–202 of the Astynomoi law where to the prohibition to pollute water coming from fountains is followed by the description of the arrest and denunciation procedures in which the *astynomoi* play an important part. The parallel, however, stops here and, given the paucity of data, I refrain from drawing other, highly speculative conclusions.

---

280 1144: Δημ̣όνους Ἀντιγόνου ἀγορανο̣[μήσας] / Περία̣νδρος Ἡγησαγόρου ἀστυν[όμησας] / Ἑρμε̣ῖ καὶ Ἀφροδίτει. 1145: Πάχης Ἀναξιθέμιδος ἀγορανομήσας Κάλλιμος Ἀριστοδήμου ἀστυνομήσας / Ἑρμεῖ καὶ Ἀφροδίτει.

281 See Vial 1985, pp. 236–237.

282 See again Vial 1985, pp. 232–237 and Stanley 1976, pp. 197–237.

283 On *agoranomoi*'s tasks see *ID* 509 and Stanley 1976.

5.2.2.4 Rhodes

Epigraphic evidence testifying to *astynomoi* also comes from Rhodes, at least for the decades between the 1st B. C. and the 1st A. D.[284] Overall they appear five times, but in three instances the texts have an honorific character and do not specify any duty they might have had.[285]

A dedication that Maiuri published in 1925 has been used to prove the importance of this magistracy in Rhodes. According to this scholar: "per il fatto che vengono qui subito dopo i ταμίαι dobbiam ritenere che gli *astynomoi* occupassero nel rango delle magistrature civili un rango assai piú elevato di quanto non ritenesse il van Gelder"[286] who, however, did not know this inscription and in his attempt to rank the *astynomoi* concluded instead that they were quite low in the local hierarchy.[287] Ranking magistrates with so little evidence is difficult but we can still try to undertake an analysis of this scanty material to better define their role. To this end, two texts may be of help: the first is *IG* XII.1, 1, the second was published by Pugliese Carratelli in the *Supplemento Epigrafico Rodio* of the SAIA in the 1950's.

IG XII.1, 1 is fragmentary and contains an unusually high number of mistakes on the stone, whose text was restored as follows:

[– – – – – – – – – – – – – –]IA[– – – – –] / [τ]ῶν ἀστυνό[μων - - - - - - -] / τον· ἔστω <δ>ὲ τῶ[ι μὲν ξένωι(?) δίκη ἐκ] / [τ]<ῶ>ν <ϑ>εῶν · ὁ δὲ δοῦλ[ος μαστιγού]/[σϑ]ω μ[ὴ] ἔλασσον πλαγ[ὰς – *numerus* –] / [..]· τὸ δὲ ψ̣ά<φι>σμα τόδε ἀν[αγράψαν]/[τ]ες τοὶ ἀστυνόμοι ἐστ[άλαν λιϑί]/[ναν] ϑέντω πρὸ τᾶν ϑυρ[ᾶν τοῦ - - , τὸ] / δὲ ἔργον ἁ[π]οδόσ[ϑων τοὶ πωλη]/[ταὶ] καϑ' ἅ κα ἀρχιτέ[κτων συγγρά]/[ψηι – – – – – – – – – – – – – – – – –][288]

The emending and restoring of the first lines is very heavy, but overall logical. The editor claimed that this is a *lex sacra*, but there is no basis for that.[289] I am not concerned with the definition of the nature of this

---

284 See Maiuri 1925, n. 20.

285 *ASAtene* 2, 1916, 124, 267; *IG* XII.I. 44; *IG* XII.I. 55; Maiuri 1925, n. 20; Pugliese Carratelli 1952–54 (*Suppl. Ep. Rodio*), n. 1.

286 See Maiuri 1925, p. 34.

287 See Van Gelder 1900, pp. 258–259.

288 LL. 4–11: "slaves should be punished with no less than [number] of lashes [...] the *astynomoi* shall set up the stele in front of the door after inscribing the decree, the *poletai* shall contract the job according to the prescription given by the architect"

289 On the definition of "sacred laws" see Lupu 2005's introduction and Dreher 2008, p. 139. Essential on the topic is the article by Parker 2004, pp. 57–71.

text; what is of interest here are the provisions for the punishments for slaves that find a parallel in the Astynomoi Law, col. IV. Finally, the text specifically says that the *astynomoi* are responsible for the setting up of the stele in a visible place. Nothing else can be inferred on their duties.

J. and L. Robert published the second document attesting to the existence of *astynomoi* in Rhodes by deciphering the picture of a stone printed in *JHS*.[290] The inscription concerns statues and votives located in the Asclepieum and more specifically intends to prevent new objects being set up on the sanctuary paths. As it is usual in these documents, provisions against offenders follow the prohibition and, after that, LL. 20–23, we read: - - - καὶ τοὶ ἀστυνόμοι, εἴ κά τις / [ἀνα]θῆι, μεθελόντω τὰ ἀναθήματα ἐς ἄλ/[λον τ]όπον· κτλ If somebody disregarded the provisions, the *astynomoi* had to move away the objects from the off-limit areas.

The clauses recorded in these two inscriptions do not provide any unusual data and allow the conclusion that the local *astynomoi* were civic magistrates who also intervened on sacred areas. They acted as a board and had routine duties such as taking care of the engraving and setting up of inscriptions or policing certain areas. I must point out that these texts cannot be securely dated since paleography is the only criterion.

In conclusion, Rhodes had a board of *astynomoi* which appears busy with routine, practical matters. There is no trace of judicial power or any activity tied to a commercial context.

5.2.3 Western and Central Anatolia

Besides Pergamon, *astynomoi* appear in several other cities of Asia Minor. For these the tendency of the scholarly community to compare them with their homonyms from Athens reaches its extreme.

Astynomoi were active in the Carian *polis* of Iasos where the evidence consists in one attestation only, now published as *I. Iasos* 1. This text is of major historical significance being concerned with the immediate

[290] See PUGLIESE CARRATELLI 1952–54 (*Suppl. Ep. Rodio*), pp. 247–249; J. and L. ROBERT *BE* 1948, n. 172. Also SOSIN 2005, pp. 133–134, n. 16 with new emendations to the text.

aftermath of the revolt against Mausolos that took place between 367/6 and 355/4.[291] This is not the place for a detailed historical discussion of this event and I limit my observations to the fact that the text, L. 10, mentions two *astynomoi* among other civil and sacred magistrates who had to put on sale the property confiscated from those who acted against Mausolos. The case described in this text is exceptional because of the events, but I assume that even under extreme circumstances the city resorted to its regular institutions and procedures (!), if only to give the appearance of normality. Assuming that this was a routine task for the local *astynomoi*, a parallel to it could be found in LL. 95–101 of the Astynomoi law where these magistrates stood by the *amphodarchai* who presided over the auction selling seized goods.[292]

In Aphrodisias an *astynomos* appears in a document that dates to the Roman period; J. Reynolds tried to set stricter chronological limits for this inscription by suggesting an "Augustan date," but the date is still uncertain.[293] The inscription preserves only a short section of what must have been an honorary decree that probably listed the numerous merits of a citizen. Among these, what stands out is his service to the *polis* in defending its privileges (or their acquisition) before an emperor.[294] The honoree held several offices during his life including that of *astynomos*. Unfortunately, none of his duties are listed. But the fact that this is recorded suggests that the office was still worthy of citation and carried some weight.

---

291 See *Syll*^{3} 169; *Iasos* 1; LAVIOSA, BA 31–32, 1985 Suppl. 47–54 (non vidi) on which see *SEG* XXXVI, 981.

292 The *astynomoi* of Alexandria might have had a similar task too, see *P. Hal.* 1, LL. 234–241 *infra*.

293 See REYNOLDS 1982, n. 41; J. and L. ROBERT *BE* 1983, n. 390.

294 See Reynolds' comment proposing to identify this outstanding member of the community with Solon son of Demetrios. This possibility is also endorsed by the Roberts in *BE*.

Kyzikos on the Hellespont had this office too.[295] Once again the evidence is limited to one, possibly two attestations of, here, only one *astynomos*. This magistrate first appears in an inscription normally dated to the first half of the 2nd century B. C., *Syll.*³ 644/645, known as the monument for Eudemos son of Nikon from Seleukia.[296] The stele records several honorary decrees for this man, who is also defined φίλος καὶ εὔνους of a king Antiochos, probably the IV.[297] The document grants proxeny and other concessions to Eudemos and in LL. 94–95 state: τὸν δὲ ἀστυνόμον ἐπιμεληθῆναι, / ὅπως ἂν ἀναγραφῆι εἰς τὴν στήλην τῶν π[ρο]ξέ[νω]ν, *i. e. astynomoi* had to set up the stele on which all these honors were recorded. In Rhodes, *IG* XII.1.1, local *astynomoi* had the same duty, but in *Syll.*³ 644/645 the magistrate's title appears in the singular. This is further confirmed by the use of the definite article in L. 93 in the same number and suggests that Kyzikos had only one *astynomos* instead of the customary board.

Recently, Kl. Hallof has published a second inscription that may attest to this magistrate in Kyzikos. This is one of several decrees with which a few cities granted *asylia* to Cos.[298] The text is fragmentary, but L. 53 records the title *astynomos* almost in its entirety. Once more this appears in the singular as the last two letters of the article in the accusative case assure. Hallof has also noted that the *astynomos* is cited in a passage of the decree where we would expect provisions for the setting up of the stele. Given the uncertainty surrounding the document, he has only restored it in the *apparatus criticus* and, as a parallel, provides the only other known inscription recording this official in Kyzikos, namely *Syll.*³ 644/645. This is all the evidence in our hands from this city; both

[295] This city was probably one of the richest and most important communities from the 4th century B. C. onward in the Greek Mediterranean, but very little work has been done on it. The most complete treatment is still HASLUCK 1910. Proper excavations have never been undertaken in the area and the few inscriptions that we have are occasional findings. Ancient sources confirm its importance, however, see STRAB. XII.8.11 = 576 C asserting that Kyzikos ἔστι δ' ἐνάμιλλος ταῖς πρώταις τῶν κατὰ τὴν Ἀσίαν ἡ πόλις μεγέθει τε καὶ κάλλει καὶ εὐνομίᾳ πρός τε εἰρήνην καὶ πόλεμον· "The city equals the first cities in Asia Minor for its dimensions, beauty, and good administration in peace and war."

[296] This is Seleukia of Cilicia or on the Kalykadnos, COHEN 1995, pp. 369–371.

[297] See SAVALLI 1998, n. 52, p. 54; CARSANA 1996, E28 and HEBERDEY-WILHELM 1896, n. 182.

[298] See HALLOF 2008, pp. 309–311; on *asylia* see RIGSBY 1996, esp. pp. 106–153 for Cos.

surviving citations agree in referring to one *astynomos* only and allow the conclusion that here this magistrate acted alone and possibly had routine duties.

Astynomoi are also attested in Cnidos, but the evidence is again rather slim. In the first half of the 2nd century B. C., three *astynomoi* dedicated a statue base to Agathe Tyche.[299] The inscription was found in 1973 and was then the first attestation of this board in Cnidos, but still did not provide any information on their actual tasks.[300]

More recently, Blümel has published a fragment of some interest:[301] ἀστυνόμοι τ[οὶ ἄρχοντες? τὰν] / χειμερινὰν ἑξάμηνον [τὰν] / ἐπὶ δαμιουργοῦ Γοργίδ[ου . . .] (names follow).

As matter of fact, this helps to restore another document, *IK Knidos* 37, whose fragmentary status and lack of paralles had left it incomplete for a long time.

]ΑΣ[ ]ΟΠΟ[/ τ]ὰν χειμερινὰν ἑξ[άμηνον? /] τ̣ὰν ἐπὶ δα. Καλλιμ̣[/] Μόσχος Ἀριστο[- - -κτλ (names follow).

Blümel has the merit of realizing that *IK Knidos* 37 and the new text are very close, which made him suggest that the first, newer inscription was probably referring to a board of *astynomoi* too. The two texts date to different centuries: the former belongs to the Hellenistic period, while the second dates to the early (?) imperial time, as paleography and prosopography seem to suggest. Unfortunately, they do not provide any direct information on the possible duties of the local *astynomoi*, but at least they tell us that in Cnidos this office lasted one semester. Their term was considerably shorter than that of the Athenian *astynomoi* for example, which could imply that their duties were also of a different nature and possibly required less "planning" and continuity.

In Ankara *astynomoi* appear four times in honorific inscriptions that date to the I and / or II century A. D.[302] Bosch commented on them thus: "Der astynomos ist der Direktor der Strassen, Bau- und Brunnen-

---

[299] See *IK Knidos* I, n. 187. See also J. and L. Robert *BE* 1974, n. 549.

[300] See Love 1973, p. 418 on pl. 74 *ph.* This scholar mentions the Athenian *astynomoi* and their duties in n. 20, an instance of the habit of using the Athenian template to explain the possible duties of this board.

[301] See Blümel 1997, pp. 406–407. Also cf. *SEG* XLIX 1431.

[302] Bosch 1967, n. 201 = Mitchell 2012, n. 127 (second half of the II A. D.); Bosch 1967, n. 202 = Mitchell 2012, n. 128 (second half of the II A. D.); Mitchell 2012, n. 129 cf. *SEG* XLVI 1626 (I or II A. D.); Bosch 1967, 262 = Mitchell

polizei, der dafür verantwortlich ist, dass die Strassen seines Bezirkes sauber und gut gehalten sind, dass die Gebäude allen baupolizeilichen Vorschriften entsprechen und die Brunnen und Wasserleitungen funktionieren und sauber sind. Es gab für jeden Bezirk einen Astynomon, die Zahl der Bezirke entsprach der Zahl der Phylen, sodass also für Ankara 12 Astynomen anzunehmen sind."[303] Bosch thus tried to explain *astynomia* in Ankara under Commodus with the duties attested in Athens for the 5th–4th century B. C.[304] Moreover, he assumed a correspondence between the number of the members of this board and the local tribes, which had been once suggested for Athens too, but without any strong foundation.[305] In Athens tribes were based on a random number of *demoi* grouped together in Trytties, but these were taken from different areas of Attica to form a tribe. Because of this, assigning an *astynomos* to each tribe would have been at best impractical since they operated in the territory. That aside, such a correspondence would have been noted in the *Athenaion Politeia*. This text only tells that five *astynomoi* were active in the Peiraeus and five in the city. The geographical criterion applied, but not in relation to tribes.

Although the evidence is very limited, it is sufficiently safe to assert that the office of *astynomia* was common in Anatolia. The role and duties of its members, however, are never specified in detail, except for Pergamon. The available data cannot support further hypotheses on their tasks, even if based on parallels such as Athens. Only the *astynomoi* from the Attalid residence-city are well known and even if it is undeniable that they resemble the Athenian magistrates in some way, this is too little to extend this statement to all other *poleis* where they were active.

2012, n. 132 (I or II A. D.). Mitchell does not comment directly on the role of these magistrates in his new corpus of the inscriptions from Ankara.

303 See Bosch 1967, p. 264.

304 Bosch seems to refer to the duties that Plato assigned to the *astynomoi* of his Magnesia, which are not always the same as those the Athenian officials had, see *supra*.

305 See Oehler *RE* 1896, colls 1870–72: "Die Zahl derselben richtete sich meinst nach der Phylen oder Unterabteilung des Volkes". The genesis of Bosch's statement is easily justifiable, namely a parallel with Athens whose ten tribes were easily equaled with 10 magistrates.

5.2.4 Black Sea

Numerous amphora stamps from cities located on the coast of the Black Sea, especially Sinope, and from the Tauric Chersonese testify to the presence of *astynomoi*.[306] The evidence does not allow us to elaborate on their tasks, but scholars have attempted to arrange it chronologically on the basis of the *astynomoi*'s names and the formulae that these short texts use.

The very numerous stamps from Sinope have been divided into six groups on the basis of the magistrates that appeared on them and the group called *astynomic* counts a very large number of examples.[307] These short texts usually contain the magistrates' names along with city symbols and the name of the amphoras' producers, which allow the dating of these *astynomic*-group stamps to the 3rd and 2nd century B. C. circa. In his study of these documents, Garlan has stressed that in Sinope the *astynomoi* practically dominate the record, although in several instances *agoranomoi* and *aisymnetai* appear too.[308] The former were the officials active in the agora and in commercial areas in general,[309] which makes their mention on an amphora stamp self-explanatory. The *aisymnetes* was Sinope's eponymous magistrate, which may justify their presence on stamps too.[310] That said, we cannot be sure why the *astynomoi* appear. Perhaps they supervised either commercial activities or legal matters in the harbor area in some capacity. *Astynomoi* and *agoranomoi* are sometimes associated, for example in Delos they appeared together in dedications to Hermes and it may be a possibility that even in Sinope they worked side by side in a commercial area.[311] Literary sources, however, never testify to any activity strictly related to commerce for *astynomoi*, but it is known that in Athens five of them operated in the harbor area of the Peiraeus, which still does not mean that they had anything to do with trade.

---

[306] The most recent findings are listed yearly in *SEG*.

[307] For the history of the studies see CONOVICI 1998, 1997; and GARLAN 2004. See J. and L. ROBERT *BE* 1952, n. 11.

[308] See GARLAN 2004, p. 6 and JEFREMOW 2003, pp. 9–14.

[309] See for example the *agoranomoi* in Delos VIAL 1985, pp. 232–235. In general STANLEY 1976 and still HÄDERLI 1886.

[310] See SHERK 1992, p. 246.

[311] See for example *IG* XI.4. 1144 and 1145 and my section on the *astynomoi* in Delos *supra*.

An additional brief note on Sinope is due after Fedoseev's recent study of the epigraphic and archaeological evidence from this city that led him to assert that Plutarch's narrative on the much debated Perikles' foundation of a clerouchy in Sinope is reliable.[312] Fedoseev holds that the institutional setting of Sinope was strongly influenced by this Athenian clerouchy and even the existence of *astynomia* was a direct consequence of it. His arguments, however, are not compelling as other explanations could be possible; for example he insists on onomastics as proof of strong Athenian presence, but names could have reached the area also through other channels, such as partly through Milesian presence or from protracted contact with Athens without implying necessarily the existence of a clerouchy.[313]

5.2.5 Macedonia and Thrace

The first and only attestation of *astynomoi* for this area comes from recently found roof-tiles that date to the 4th–3rd century B. C. Adam-Veleni is responsible for their first publication in which she has, rightly, stated that their presence vouches for the existence of a well-developed urban center in the area by modern Vrasna (?), ancient Bormiskos.[314] Given the type of evidence, however, nothing else on their duties or role can be said.

Finally, a funerary inscription from Philippopolis dated to the Roman time testifies to an *astynomos*. Here too we can only conclude that the office existed and that this office had some significance if it was so recorded.[315]

---

312 See FEDOSEEV 2002, esp. p. 196; also IDEM 2003 in Russian with summary in English, see also *SEG* LIII, 1432. According to Plutarch's testimony in PLUT. *Per*. 20. 2: Σινωπεῦσι δὲ τρισκαίδεκα ναῦς ἀπέλιπε μετὰ Λαμάχου ἐπὶ Τιμησίλεων τύραννον. ἐκπεσόντος δὲ τούτου καὶ τῶν ἑταίρων ἐψηφίσατο πλεῖν εἰς Σινώπην Ἀθηναίων ἐθελοντὰς ἑξακοσίους καὶ συγκατοικεῖν Σινωπεῦσι, νειμαμένους οἰκίας καὶ χώραν ἣν πρότερον οἱ τύραννοι κατεῖχον.

313 See FEDOSEEV 2002, pp. 189–201. A critical view on this clerouchy in MATTINGLY 1996, pp. 151–156 and FERRARESE 1974, pp. 7–19. Fedoseev discusses their objections, but does not offer compelling arguments against those.

314 See ADAM – VELENI 1999, pp. 8–9, see *SEG* XLV, 743. Newly published material from Demetrias in Thessaly in FURTWÄNGLER 2006.

315 See *IG Bulg.* III 1023 and *SEG* XLVI, 2310.

5.3 The *Astynomikos nomos* of the *Dikaiomata*, P. Hal. 1

LL. 234–241 of *P.Hal.* 1 record a section on security as a pledge, ἐνεχυρασία, a theme upon which the Astynomoi law touches too. Unfortunately, this papyrus, which preserves passages of different regulations, possibly from Alexandria, is too fragmentary and does not provide us with a context.[316] Still, the lines dealing with *enechyrasia* deserve a brief discussion:

Θεσμοφυλακ β´

(235) ἐνεχυρασία καὶ . πο. . . . . [ἐὰ]ν δὲ περὶ τ̣[. . . . . . . μὴ ἐξέστω] / ἐνεχυράζειν μηδὲ ὅ<u>ταν</u> τις ἀποθά[νηι. . . . .] / (237) κατὰ τὸν νό<u>μ</u>ον ἀ[σ]<u>τυνο</u>[μ]ικὸν [. . . . .] / μηδὲ ἵππον <u>δ</u>ημοσιευ[έτω]σαν. [ἐ]ὰν δέ τις ἐ[νεχυράσηι, ἀναγρα]/φέτωσαν οἱ θεσμοφύλακ[ες] τὴ[ν] ἐνεχυρασί[αν]. [ὡς δὲ ἂν ἥλιος] / (240) δύηι, μηδὲ εἷς ἐνεχυρα<u>ζ</u>[έ]τω μηδὲ πρὶν ἥ[λιον ἀνατέλλειν],/ ἢ [ὑ]πόδικοι ἔστωσαν οἱ η[νεχ⟨υρακ⟩ότ]ες τῆς ψευδε[νεχυρασίας][317]

Between lacunae, in L. 237 we learn of the existence of specific procedures listed in an *astynomikos nomos*. This allows the conclusion that Alexandria must have had *astynomoi* and a law comparable to that from Pergamon that regulated their duties.[318] The text implies also that the *astynomoi* were involved in *enechyrasia* at least at some level. In this regard it is worth recalling the section of the Astynomoi law establishing that the *astynomoi* played a (passive) part in the confiscation of belongings to residents who neglected their cleaning duties by not paying their dues, LL. 95–101, which suggest that these magistrates were routinely involved in repossession procedures. An additional parallel to this also comes from Iasos where they were to sell confiscated property of Mausolos' opponents.[319] Even if this is only sporadically attested, it is possible that in certain cities the *astynomoi* were routinely involved in repossessions and auction of repossessed goods.

---

316 A comment in *Dikaiomata* 1913, pp. 134–139.

317 Text from *Dikaiomata* 1913, p. 134; "Pledging and [...] it shall not be allowed taking as a pledge nor when one has passed away [...] according to the *astynomikos nomos* nor shall one repossess a horse. If one takes a pledge, the *thesmopylakes* shall register that. Nobody shall take a pledge after the sun has gone down, or before sunrise. Those who do it are liable to be subject to justice because of a wrongly taken pledge."

318 See *Dikaiomata* 1913, esp. p. 40 and pp. 134–139.

319 See *supra* the section on Iasos in Western Anatolia.

5.4 Conclusion

The evidence I have presented in these pages is all we have on *astynomoi* in the Greek World, which is not as much as we would like. Clearly, our major sources of information come from Athens and Pergamon where the duties of these magistrates appear to be quite similar, although for the first the bulk of the evidence comes from the 4th century B. C. and for Pergamon we have a text that dates to the 2nd century B. C. inscribed on a 2nd century A. D. stone. The duties of these magistrates are close in spite of chronology, but whether all attested duties (for example) can be extended to all other communities in which *astynomoi* appear is questionable. The size of a city seems to have been an important factor in the determination of the tasks magistrates had to perform, as Tenos shows and as Aristotle observed too. Small communities tended to concentrate more tasks in the hands of a magistrate, while in bigger cities there was the tendency to specialize. This alone should warn one against dangerous generalization and recommend a more cautious approach: Athenian *astynomia* cannot have been a model for all other cities and extending its tasks to the members of the homonymous office all over the Mediterranean is methodologically unsound.

6 Perspectives: *Astynomoi* in the Greek World and Other Magistrates with Comparable Duties

However different, the duties attested for *astynomoi* all over the Mediterranean seem to respond to the basic needs of a city. It is possible, as *P.Hal.* 1 seems to suggest, that all *poleis* with *astynomoi* had an *astynomikos nomos* to regulate their activity. The surviving evidence, however, is sparse and for several towns we have to make do with a handful of honorific inscriptions that often do not provide helpful data.

I have stressed repeatedly that the Athenian *astynomia* has become a template for this magistracy, but in a few cases scholarship has extended the duties of these *astynomoi* to other towns from which we hardly have telling evidence. A good example is Cnidos of whom we know no more than they existed. Still, Love has assimilated them to the Athenian ones, even though it is now known with certainty that they were only in charge for 6 months. This quick turn-around may or may not have been important for assigning duties, but it is a factor we have to consider in any general evaluation.

Yet, in spite of the limitations imposed by the evidence, what is left seems to point to a general pattern: the *astynomoi* policed public infrastructures, sometimes even private properties and could have limited judicial tasks. Inscriptions testify to routine duties too: in Rhodes and Kyzikos they were in charge of setting up stele following the passing of a decree; or, still in Rhodes, they had to move votive objects from overcrowded sacred areas. These may appear trivial responsibilities, but show that these officials were active in town and part of everyday life. In several areas they had the power to initiate a judicial process and took care of lesser matters directly, but had to refer more serious problems to higher authorities, which may be seen as a sign of low rank. The same evidence, however, could be read in exactly the opposite way: their constant presence and involvement in numerous daily activities could have increased their importance and visibility because they were informed on many, crucial mechanisms that regulated and assured the well functioning of city-life. The best example is the *isopoliteia* treaty between Keos and Histiaea, where we learn that the citizens of Histiaea in Keos could refer to the *astynomoi* in cases of necessity. This suggests that they had a central role in the administration and life of the city. Speculating on other, more specific tasks is hard. Evidence of their involvement in, for example, building policy and cleaning, other than in Pergamon, comes only from Athens. Yet Adam-Veleni's statement that their attestation assures the existence of a well-developed urban area is certainly accurate. As Sartori has suggested, the *astynomoi* belong to a "generica categoria di magistrati" reflecting the needs of an urban community.[320] These were the *astynomoi*: local, civic magistrates who dealt with everyday matters and contributed to the smooth running of an urban centre and because of this they can be considered all the more important. Finally, many inscriptions reveal their constant involvement in sacred affairs, even if always in relation to administrative matters. For this reason Klingenberg dubbed them "Fest-sakral Polizei," largely forgetting their secular duties.

A last matter pertains to magistrates with different titles, but similar responsibilities. In his *RE* article, Oehler observed that each city must have had officials attending to daily duties no matter what they were called.[321] *Astynomoi* aside, he noted the title of three such magistrates: the *polianomoi* in Heraklea in Magna Graecia and Syracuse, the *telearchos* attested in Thebes and the *pateres* who are mentioned once in Corinth.[322] The parallel with the *polianomoi* is the only one that can be substantiated by the evidence, while for the other two magistracies the data is too scanty. A quick review of the evidence for the *polianomoi* could help determine whether this parallel is relevant.

The *polianomoi*

The *polianomoi* appear a few times and in different places, namely Herakleia in Magna Graecia, Syracuse, perhaps Sparta, and in the *chora* of Cyrene.

The two famous tables from Herakleia provide the bulk of the evidence.[323] These officials appear several times in the first table,[324] in the section devoted to the letting of Dionysus' land. The text dates to the

---

320 Sartori 1967, pp. 60–61.
321 Oehler *RE* 1896, coll. 1870–72.
322 *Telearchoi* in Plut. *Praec. Ger. Reip.* 811b; for the *pateres* see Diog. Laert. VI. 78.
323 Uguzzoni – Ghinatti 1968; Sartori 1967; Sartori 1965.
324 I.96; 104–105; 110; 117; 124; 134; 164–165; 177–178.

end of the 4th century B. C.,[325] when the city probably enjoyed a period of freedom and decided to regulate the occupation of the land that had been taken illegally in a moment of political chaos. The *polianomoi* had an active role in these proceedings since they rented out the plots, wrote contracts and were responsible for the collection of eventual fines from those who were late with their rent.[326] Moreover, they had to assure that the new rules were enforced with the help of ten citizens chosen among the People. From these texts we gather that the *polianomoi* had multiple duties sometimes resembling those of the *astynomoi* to the point that Ghinatti suggested that they were almost the same office only with a different name. A remark by Sartori is of interest too: "si conoscono, per esempio, gli astinomi di numerose città, i quali sembrano aver avuto peró compiti meno ampi (*rispetto ai polianomi*)" but also that the reference to the *astynomoi* "indica solamente la categoria generale di magistrati".[327] It is true that we ought to speak of a "general category" of magistrates in charge of everyday duties for a smooth running of the life of a *polis*, but the evidence contradicts the first part of Sartori's statement, namely Herakleia's *polianomoi* did not have more responsibilities than the *astynomoi* in Pergamon or Athens. The detailed character of the procedures described by the tables from Herakleia certainly conveys this impression, while the description of the *astynomoi'* duties we have is more general, but not necessarily less labor-intensive and certainly not confined to a clearly-set period of time.

An inscription from the *chora* of Cyrene records the presence of *polianomoi* in the 1st century B. C.[328] Only the second half of the text is preserved, but we can still determine that this was an honorific decree for an *euergetes*. LL. 17–20 mention *polianomoi*:

. . .τοὶ δὲ πολιανό/μοι τὸ ψάφισμα ἐγγραψάτωσαν / εὐσάμως ἐς τὰν κοινὰν τὰν / τᾶ[ς] κῶμας συνθήκαν . . .

These magistrates were responsible for the publication of the text so that, says the subsequent hortative clause, those passing by would see that the community rewarded its benefactors. These lines seem ambitious for a small community 14 km away from Cyrene, still through them we

325 See Arangio Ruiz-Olivieri 1925, n. 1.
326 Uguzzoni – Ghinatti 1968, p. 154.
327 Sartori 1967, pp. 60–61.
328 Laronde 1987, pp. 334–336 also in *SEG* IX. 354.

learn that it had local magistrates among which the *polianomoi*. It is appropriate here to recall that in Rhodes and Kyzikos *astynomoi* performed the same task: just like *astynomoi*, *polianomoi* dealt with routine activities.

The evidence for *astynomoi* testifies that they were concerned with sacred events too, which is not attested, except in restoration, for the *polianomoi*. Beattie suggested that a text from Sparta, *IG* V.1 722,[329] attests to it. This dates to the archaic period and Beattie calls it a *lex sacra*. The exact role of the *polianomos,* which appears only in an uncertain restoration, is unclear, but possibly should have to do with a cult.[330] This inscription, however, is extremely fragmentary and Bettie's restoration equally uncertain.

This is all the evidence on *polianomia*. Certainly, both *polianomia* and *astynomia* are attested more or less securely for a rather long period and had a plurality of duties that always pertain to the daily life of a city in the secular and perhaps sacred sphere. The *polianomoi* are not as well known as the *astynomoi,* but in Herakleia and near Cyrene seem to have been invested with duties pertaining to the smooth running of the community. A comparison with the *astynomoi* on this thin basis seems to me quite daring and indeed hardly possible, but I suggest that we retain Sartori's idea of the existence of a general category of officials that could take different names. Each city had tasks that had to be necessarily carried out and different magistrates with a range of daily but crucial duties existed all over the Mediterranean.

---

329 Beattie 1951, esp. p. 57, see also Robert *BE* 1951, n. 119.

330 Other sources are Pl., *Epist*. 3. 363; Cass. Dio. 43. 28, 48, but they do not add anything new. See Sartori 1967, p. 61.

7 The Astynomoi Law and its Value

With these pages I have tried to provide a supplement to Klaffenbach's edition by including the new evidence, often of archeological and epigraphic nature that has emerged since 1954. I already had occasion to say that this is not a philological commentary but rather an analysis of the content in the light of the progress of the past century on part of scholarship in different fields. The Attalid institutions are now much better known and even if it is still difficult to determine why the *epi tcs poleos* was collaborating with the *strategoi* in this text, now we know at least who the *epi tes poleos* was and that the civic *strategoi* were not royal appointees. I could go on, but this is not the place to summarize the entire commentary. Before concluding, however, a lingering question must be addressed, namely that pertaining to the significance of the Astynomoi law in the 2nd century A. D. or, in other words, whether we can pin point or suggest the reason behind its re-engraving and public display three centuries after the actual law had been enacted. Scholarship has tackled this query many times and indeed after the debate on chronology was exhausted, the problem of the re-publication became central. Two theses have been proposed over the years and, since Klaffenbach's edition, supporters of both have presented arguments *pro* and *contra* each of them. Klaffenbach's opinion stated that the inscription was only a *monumentum*, thus depriving the inscribed regulation of any practical value, since it it would simply have reflected the antiquarian interests of the century. The other opinion strongly opposed this view by asserting instead that the only reason to have such a document re-inscribed was its continued applicability. This last view has won over the majority of supporters among whom I count myself.

That cities retained their own institutions under Rome is largely accepted and so is their progressive adjustment to the new political situation thanks to the development of a diplomatic language and tools that allowed communication with the new forms of authority.[331] Political changes notwithstanding, cities had basic administrative and maintainance needs that were a-political and timeless. The content of the

[331] The work by MA 2000 is an important methodological reference even if it deals with pre-Apameia issues.

Astynomoi law responded to them too and for this reason it is more than likely that such regulation suited the needs of a city in the 2nd A. D. as much as it did in the 2nd B. C. A scholar who treated this problem and reached these conclusions well before I did is M. Amelotti who wrote in 2001: "Sull'opinione che si trattasse di una riproduzione priva di scopi pratici, rispondente al gusto arcaicizzante dell'epoca, ha prevalso quella di una permanenza in vigore della legge sotto i Romani. Ciò è apparso anche a me convincente sia perché quel complesso di norme di polizia municipale rispondeva, pur con impliciti aggiornamenti, ad esigenze sempre attuali in una città, sia perché esso non presentava alcun carattere politico, incompatibile con l'organizzazione romana della provincia d'Asia."[332] That this was a "Royal Law" must have helped too, especially if it really had been re-engraved under Hadrian, as many scholars like to think.[333] The 2nd century A. D. was a time when the recovery of the past was looked upon with favor; it has been even suggested that re-inscribing such a document could have been part of a larger attempt to establish a relation between the Golden Age of Pergamon under Eumenes II and the revived prosperity of the city under Hadrian.[334] This is not unparallelled in Hadrian's *modus operandi*, as for example a recent study on the Athenian oil law by K. Harter-Uibopuu shows.[335] According to her, Hadrian's interventions on local laws were conducted so as "to remind the Athenians of the classical roots of their system of procedure." This, however, was done so as he could claim for himself a place among the "important Athenian nomothetai who empowered the Athenian people."[336] This is an example of the imperial attitude and shows the emperor's sensitivity towards subject cities and their pride. But this concerns Athens, while the presence and the relation that Hadrian had with Pergamon is a different and distictly less attested matter. Nevertheless, it seems plausible that this regulation was re-inscribed because it was still applicable and possibly Hadrian, or another emperor, had very little to do with it. Certainly, a few details would have seemed anachronistic, including several

332 See Amelotti 2001, p. 225, see also idem 1958.

333 See *supra*.

334 Still the law may have been enacted by one the last two Attalid kings, see *supra* p. 15, n. 13.

335 See Harter-Uibopuu 2008.

336 See Harter-Uibopuu 2008, p. 138.

of the magistrates or the amounts for fines, but this should not prevent us from thinking that the general rules could still be applied.[337]

The Astynomoi law is a good example of institutional continuity within a *polis*, but, at the same time, it may be a sign of a city's attempt to retain its identity in a changed world by recovering pieces of the past that were still serviceable. If past regulations could and would still be applied, the *polis* as community and civic entity proved that it had something to contribute in any century. This may seem a compromise between the two theses that have long opposed each other, but a closer look shows they are not mutually exclusive. The historical circumstances and the cultural atmosphere of the 2nd century A. D. with its attention to and cult of the past cannot be forgotten. At the same time, however, the elite that encouraged this cult took part in the life of the new institutions and politics, as the example of Claudius Charax shows.[338] These two aspects could be reconciled and should not be considered a sign of a political-social-legistative-schizophrenia. More properly, this combination could be read as a political statement, the pride of belonging to a community with an important history that was conscious of its new, drastically reduced role, but still proud of its past and its identity.

---

[337] See MARTINI 1999 on the XII Tables. A recently published law on irrigation from Roman Spain that dates to the age of Hadrian contains general provisions in part resembling those of the Astynomoi law. This to say that common sense, along with certain expectations is not time sensitive. See BELTRÁN LLORIS 2006.

[338] See again ANDREI 1984.

8 Appendix: the *Astynomikos Monobiblos*

A curious passage from the so-called ἀστυνομικὸν βιβλίον ἕν that the *Digest* records in *D.* 43.10.1 under the contested paternity of Papinian describes in detail the duties of *astynomoi* of non-specified provenance.[339] This Greek text should date to the period of the Severii and survives in isolation, without any context that could help answer specific questions on the identity or chronology of these *astynomoi*. I do not intend to discuss the issue of the attribution that has caused a heated debate already, instead my focus is the content of the text that reads almost as a summary of the sources on the *astynomoi* that I have analyzed in my entire commentary.

> ἐκ τοῦ ἀστυνομικοῦ μονοβίβλου τοῦ Παπινιανοῦ. Οἱ ἀστυνομικοὶ ἐπιμελείσθωσαν τῶν κατὰ τὴν πόλιν ὁδῶν, ὅπως ἂν ὁμαλισθῶσιν καὶ τὰ ῥεύματα μὴ βλάπτῃ τὰς οἰκίας καὶ γέφυραι ὦσιν οὗ ἂν δέῃ. ἐπιμελείσθωσαν δὲ ὅπως οἱ ἴδιοι τοῖχοι ἢ τῶν ἄλλων ἢ τῶν περὶ τὰς οἰκίας ἃ εἰς τὴν ὁδὸν φέρει μὴ σφαλερὰ ᾖ, ἵνα ὡς δεῖ καθαιρῶσιν οἱ δεσπόται τῶν οἰκιῶν καὶ ἐπισκευάζωσιν. ἐὰν δὲ μὴ καθαιρῶσιν μηδὲ ἐπισκευάζωσιν, ζημιούτωσαν αὐτούς, ἕως ἂν ἀσφαλῆ ποιῶσιν. ἐπιμελείσθωσαν δὲ ὅπως μηδεὶς ὀρύσσῃ τὰς ὁδοὺς μηδὲ χωννύῃ μηδὲ κτίσῃ εἰς τὰς ὁδοὺς μηδέν· εἰ δὲ μή, ὁ μὲν δοῦλος ὑπὸ τοῦ ἐντύχοντος μαστιγούσθω, ὁ δὲ ἐλεύθερος ἐνδεικνύσθω τοῖς ἀστυνόμοις, οἱ δὲ ἀστυνόμοι ζημιούτωσαν κατὰ τὸν νόμον καὶ τὸ γεγονὸς καταλυέτωσαν. ἐπισκευάζειν δὲ τὰς ὁδοὺς τὰς δημοσίας κατὰ τὴν ἑαυτοῦ οἰκίαν ἕκαστον καὶ τὰς ὑδρορρόας ἐκκαθαίρειν τάς ἐκ τοῦ ὑπαιθρίου καὶ ἐπισκευάζειν οὕτως, ὡς ἂν μὴ κωλύῃ ἅμαξαν ἐπιέναι. ὅσοι δὲ μισθωσάμενοι οἰκοῦσιν, ἐὰν δὲ μὴ ἐπισκευάσῃ ὁ δεσπότης,

339 *Dig.* 43.10.1. See Giuffré 1976 and Martini forthcoming acts of the XV conference of the Accademia Romanistica Constantiniana. The article can be downloaded, courtesy of the author, from www.ledonline.it/rivistadirittoromano. Paternity is debated and many scholars deny it to Papinian. Recently, Martini had argued persuasively for this thesis thus, p. 7: "Ma francamente resta difficile credere che Papiniano potesse essersi messo a raccogliere leggi greche. Sarebbe più probabile che qualcuno in epoca tarda quando andavano di moda compendi giuridici attribuiti a giuristi classici come Paolo e Ulpiano, avessero voluto dare una paternità autorevole a un volumetto recante appunto disposizioni greche, *ancora vigenti nel mondo romano*" (italics mine). This opinion shares Migliardi Zingale 2009, esp. pp. 818–819.

αὐτοὶ ἐπισκευάσαντες ὑπολογιζέσθωσαν τὸ ἀνάλωμα κατὰ τὸν μισθόν. ἐπιμελείσθωσαν δὲ καὶ ὅπως πρὸ τῶν ἐργαστηρίων μηδὲν προκείμενον ᾖ, πλὴν ἐὰν κναφεὺς ἱμάτια ψύγῃ ἢ τέκτων τροχοὺς ἔξω τιθῇ· τιθέσθωσαν δὲ καὶ οὗτοι, ὥστε μὴ κωλύειν ἅμαξαν βαδίζειν. Μὴ ἐάτωσαν δὲ μηδὲ μάχεσθαι ἐν ταῖς ὁδοῖς μηδὲ κόπρον ἐκβάλλειν μηδὲ νεκρὰ μηδὲ δέρματα ῥίπτειν.

The *astynomoi* shall take care of the streets that run within the *polis*, so that their paving is all even and streams of water will not damage houses, also they should see that there are bridges where they should be. They shall see that private walls or those of others or those that surround houses whichever face on the street should not be about to fall, and that the owners of houses clean and maintain them properly if the walls require this. If they do not clean or repair, they shall fine them, until they secure these structures. They shall also see that nobody digs in the streets or throws or builds anything on them. If they do, if it is a slave he shall be whipped by the one who catches him, if he is a free man he should be denounced to the *astynomoi* and these should fine him according to the law and repair the damages. They shall see that the public streets around each resident's house are clean and that the channels coming from the courtyards are clean and arrange so that they would not hinder the passage of a carriage. For those who live in rented houses, if the owner does not repair (what has to be repaired), they themselves should do so by deducting the amount paid from the rent. Also they shall see that nothing is placed in front of a shop, except for when a fuller leaves clothes outside to dry or a wood worker wheels. They should arrange their property though, so that they would not hinder the passage of a carriage. They should not allow fighting in the streets nor that dung or corpses or skins be thrown there.

The numerous duties that the *astynomoi* had to attend to and that appear in these lines are already amply attested in the Attalid *prostagma* and in several of the Athenian sources on this office. For example, one of the main preoccupations of the legislator concerns streets and their maintenance. These must be passable at all times and their paving must be smooth and not subject to citizens' abuse. They should not dig in or throw anything on the streets, as the Astynomoi law also prescribed in col. II LL. 72–76 or the *Ath. Pol.* 50.2 does too by recommending that the *astynomoi* stop residents from building on public streets. The passage of the Astynomoi law has also shown the city's clear concern for open conduits and the damage that these could cause. It was my hypothesis that this preoccupation was mostly tied to the local traffic and *Dig.* 43.10.1 suggests this too by stating: ἐπισκευάζειν δὲ τὰς ὁδοὺς τὰς δημοσίας κατὰ τὴν ἑαυτοῦ οἰκίαν ἕκαστον καὶ τὰς ὑδρορρόας ἐκκαθαίρειν τάς ἐκ τοῦ ὑπαιθρίου καὶ ἐπισκευάζειν οὕτως, ὡς ἂν μὴ κωλύῃ ἅμαξαν ἐπιέναι. Moreover, in this and the subsequent section another point in common with the law from Pergamon emerges, namely the responsibility that the owner of a property shared with the city and its officials in the attempt to preserve the good state of its infrastructures.

I could list other similarities between this passage, Pergamon's law and the evidence from Athens, but I think that this suffices to show that, just like these documents, *D.* 43.10.1 regulates common behaviors and needs of a city.[340] The *astynomoi,* or other magistrates, were the community's agents and in this capacity implemented its rules to safeguard the integrity and interest of its infrastructures. This does not mean that chronology should be disregarded. Chronology *is* a worry, as the case of the dedication from Athens on the *sekoma* (*IG* II^2 3939 + 2878) should reveal.[341] Still the similarities of the duties for *astynomoi* thoughout the century is indeed striking. The best way to conclude is to return to the beginning of this work and cite again D. Hennig's words for which: "Wie der D. 43.10.21 zitierte Auszug aus dem in griechischer Sprache verfaßten ἀστυνομικὸς μονόβιβλος Papinians zeigt, hatte sich, wie nicht anders zu erwarten, in severischer Zeit in diesem Bereich nichts Grundsätzliches geändert."[342] Properly maintaining a city meant attending to basic needs that are timeless. Each community must have had magistrates in charge of these, whatever their title was, but at the same time the size and location of a community could determine a different division of labor among its officials. For this reason, even if a pattern

340 See AMELOTTI 2001, p. 225 and my conclusions *supra.*

341 See *supra.*

342 HENNIG 1995, p. 236. See *supra.*

can be found in the role and duties of such magistrates, applying one model to every community is a risky approach.

9 Corpora and Epigraphic Reference Works

AGER 1996: S. AGER, *Interstate Arbitrations in the Greek World, 337–390 B. C.*, Berkeley 1996.

ARANGIO RUIZ and OLIVIERI 1925: V. ARANGIO RUIZ and A. OLIVIERI, *Inscriptiones Graecae Siciliae et Infimae Italiae ad Ius pertinentes*, Milan 1925.

AvP VIII: M. FRÄNKEL, *Die Inschriften von Pergamon vol. VIII, 1–2*, Berlin 1890 and 1895.

AvP VIII. 3: CH. HABICHT, *Die Inschriften des Asklepieions, mit einem Beitrag von M Wörrle, VIII 3*, Berlin 1969.

BE: Bulletin Epigraphique.

BOSCH 1967: E. BOSCH, *Quellen zur Geschichte der Stadt Ankara im Altertum*, Ankara 1967.

CRAWFORD 1996: M. CRAWFORD, *Roman Statutes* (ed.), London 1996.

Dikaiomata: P. Halle, "Graeca Halensis", Dikaiomata, Auszüge aus Alexandrinischen Gesetzen u. Verordnungen in einem Papyrus des Phil. Sem. der Univ. Halle mit einem Anhang weiterer Papyri derselben Sammlung, Berlin 1913.

Stephanus: H. ESTIENNE, *Thesarus grecae linguae*, I–IX, tertio ediderunt C. B. HASE – G. DINDORF(IUS) – L. DINDORF(IUS), Graz 1954.

IC: M. GUARDUCCI, *Inscriptiones Creticae, opera et consilio Friderici Halbherr collectae*, Rome 1935–1950.

IG: *Inscriptiones Graecae.*

IG Bulg.: Inscriptiones Graecae in Bulgaria repertae (1956–1966)

I. Didyma: TH. WIEGAND, *Didyma*, Berlin 1958.

I. Ephesos: H. WANKEL, *Die Inschriften von Ephesos*, Bonn 1979.

I. Iasos: W. BLUEMEL, *Inschriften von Iasos I – II,* Bonn 1985.

I. von Knidos: W. BLUEMEL, *Inschriften von Knidos I*, Bonn 1982.

I. Magn.: O. KERN, *Die Inschriften von Magnesia am Maeander,* Berlin 1900.

I. Pr.: F. HILLER VON GAERTRINGEN, *Die Inschriften von Priene*, Berlin 1906.

KOERNER 1993: R. KOERNER, *Inschriftlische Gesetzetexte der frühen griechischen Polis aus dem Nachlaß von Reinhard Koerner*, Cologne 1993.

LSAM: F. Sokolowski, *Lois sacrées de l'Asie Mineure*, Paris 1955.

LSCG: F. Sokolowski, *Lois sacrées des cités grecques*, Paris 1969.

LSS: F. Sokolowski, *Lois sacrées des cités grecques. Supplément*, Paris 1962.

Maiuri: A. Maiuri, *Nuova silloge epigrafica di Rodi e Cos*, Firenze 1925.

Mitchell 2012: *The Greek and Latin Inscriptions of Ankara (Ankyra). Vol. I From Augustus to the End of the Third Century A. D.*, Edd. St. Mitchell and D. French, Vestigia 62, Munich 2012.

OGIS: W. Dittenberger, *Orientis graeci inscriptiones selectae. Supplementum Sylloges inscriptionum graecarum,* Lipsia 1903–1905.

Oliver 1989: J. H. Oliver, *Greek Constitutions of Early Roman Emperors from Inscriptions and Papyri,* Philadelphia 1989.

Petrakos 1997: B. C. Petrakos, *ΟΙ ΕΠΙΓΡΑΦΕΣ ΤΟΥ ΩΡΩΠΟΥ*, Athens 1997.

Pugliese Carratelli 1952–1954, *Suppl. Ep. Rodio*: G. Pugliese Carratelli, "Supplemento Epigrafico Rodio," *Annuario della SAIA* 14–16, 1952–1954, pp. 247–316.

Rhodes and Osborne 2003: P. J. Rhodes and R. Osborne, *Greek Historical Inscriptions 404–323 B. C.*, Oxford 2003.

SEG: Supplementum Epigraphicum Graecum.

StV: H. Bengston, *Die Staatsverträge des Altertums*, Munich 1962–1975.

Syll.³: W. Dittenberger, *Sylloge Inscriptionum Graecarum,* Hildesheim 1915–1924.

Thür – Taubner *IPArk:* G. Thür and H. Taeubner, *Prozessrechtliche Inschriften der griechischen Poleis,* Vienna 1994.

Welles *RC*: C. B. Welles, *Royal Correspondence in the Hellenistic Period. A Study on Greek Epigraphy*, Yale U.P. 1934.

10 Bibliography

P. Adam-Veleni, "ΕΠΙΓΡΑΦΙΚΕΣ ΜΑΡΤΥΡΙΕΣ ΑΠΟ ΒΡΕΣΝΑ Ν. ΘΕΣΣΑΛΟΝΙΚΗ," in *Ancient Macedonia VI, Papers read at the Sixth International Symposium held in Thessaloniki, October 15–19 1996*, Thessaloniki 1999, pp. 5–14.

R. E. Allen, *The Attalid Kingdom. A Constitutional History*, Oxford 1983.

Idem, "Attalos I and Aigina," *ABSA* 66, 1971, pp. 1–12.

M. Amelotti, "Leggi greche in diritto romano," in *Symposion* 1997, ed. by Cantarella and Thür, Vienna 2001, pp. 225–234.

Idem "L'epigrafe di Pergamo sugli ASTUNOMOI e il problema della recezione di leggi straniere nell'ordinamento giuridico romano,"*SDHI* 24, 1958, pp. 80–111.

O. Andrei, *A. Claudius Charax di Pergamo. Interessi antiquari e antichità cittadine nell'età degli Antonini,* Bologna 1984.

G. Argoud, "Construction d'un 'aqueduc grec' aux frontièrs de l'Attique (Oropos)," in *Journées d'Études sur les aqueducs Romains, Tagung über römische Wasserversorgungsanlagen, Lyon 26–28 Mai 1977*, ed. by Bouchet, Lyon 1983, pp. 1–11.

Ch. Armoni, "PSI Com. 11: ein seltenes Exemplar einer Exomosie," *ZPE* 154, 2005, pp. 214–216.

W. Aylward, "Security, *Synoikismos*, and *Koinon* as Determinants for Troad Housing in Classical and Hellenistic Times," in *Ancient Greek Houses and Households, Chronological, Regional and Social Diversity*, edd. by Ault and Nevett 2005, Philadelphia, pp. 36–53.

A. Aymard, *Études d'histoire ancienne*, Paris 1967.

E. Badian, "History from 'Square Brackets'," *ZPE* 79, 1989, pp. 59–70.

R. Bagnall, *The Administration of the Ptolemaic Possessions outside Egypt*, Leiden 1976.

A. J. Beattie, "An early Laconian *Lex Sacra,*" *CQ* New Series 1, 1951, pp. 46–58.

J. Beloch, *Die Bevölkerung der griechisch-römischen Welt,* Leipzig 1886.

F. Beltrán Lloris, "An Irrigation Decree from Roman Spain: the *Lex Rivi Hiberiensis*," *JRS* 96, 2006, pp. 147–197.

B. Bergquist, *Herakles on Thasos. The archaeological, literary and epigraphic Evidence for his Sanctuary, Status and Cult Reconsidered*, Uppsala 1973.

A. Bingen, "Review on Klaffenbach, Die Astynomeninschrift von Pergamon," *Ant. Class.* 24, 1955, pp. 254–255.

W. Blümel, "Neue Inschriften aus Karien II: Mylasa und Umgebung," *EA* 37, 2004, pp. 1–42.

Idem, "Epigraphische Forschungen im Westen Kariens," *AST* 16, 1, 1997, pp. 403–407.

M. T. Boatwright, *Hadrian and the Cities of the Roman Empire*, Princeton 2000.

C. H. Bohtz and W. D. Albert, "Die Antike Straße zur Akropolis von Pergamon," *AA* 1975, pp. 471–529.

J. du Bouchet, "Quartiers, îlots et rues: remarques sur ΑΜΦΟΔΟΝ," *RPh* 78, 2004, pp. 43–55.

B. Bravo, "Sûlan, Représailles et Justice privée contre des étrangers dans les cités grecques (Étude du vocabulaire et des institutions)," ASNP 10, 2, 1980, pp. 675–987.

W. Brinker, *Ein Beitrag zur Frage der Wasserversorgung früher Städte*, Diss. TA Braunschweig 1990.

Idem, "Die Zisternen von Pergamon im Licht der Astynomeninschrift," in *Vorträge der Tagung "Geschichtliche Wasserbauten in Ägypten", Kairo, 10. bis 17. Februar*, ed. by Garbrecht, (Mitteilungen 86), Braunschweig, 1986, pp. 1–18.

B. Brugi, "L'ambitus e il paries communis nella storia e nel sistema del diritto romano," *Rivista italiana per le scienze giuridiche* 1887, 4, pp. 161–212 and 363–407.

P. Brun, "L'île de Kéos et ses cités au IVe siècle AV J.C.," *ZPE* 76, 1989, pp. 121–138.

Ph. Bruneau, "L'esclavage à Délos," in *Mélanges Pierre Lévêque. III. Anthropologie et société*, edd. by Mactoux and Geny, Paris 1989, pp. 41–52.

S. Bussi, *Economia e demografia della schiavitù in Asia Minore Ellenistico-Romana*, Milano 2001.

G. Cardinali, *Il Regno di Pergamo. Ricerche di storia e di diritto pubblico*, Torino 1906.

L. CAPDETREY, *Le pouvoir séleucide. Territoire, administration, finances d'un royaume hellénistique (312–129 avant J.-C.)*, Rennes 2007.

CH. CARSANA, *Le dirigenze cittadine nello stato seleucidico,* Como 1996.

C. CAREY, "The Witness's *Exomosia* in the Athenian Courts," *CQ* 45.1, 1995, pp. 114–119.

G. CASA, "Giuro di no. Note a PSI com. VI 11," in *Studi Ellenistici* XX Pisa 2008, pp. 427–454.

C. CHANDEZON, *L'élevage en Grèce (fin V^e-fin Ier s. a.C.). L'apport des sourcés épigraphiques,* Pessac 2003.

IDEM, "Foires et panégyries dans le mond grec classique et hellénistique," *REG* 113, 2000, pp. 70–100.

TH. CHATELAIN, "Assèchement et bonification des terres dans l'Antiquité grecque. L'exemple Du lac de Ptéchai à Érétrie : aspcts terminologiques et techniques," in *Irrigation et drainage dans l'Antiquité, qanāts et canalisations souterraines en Iran, en Egypte et en Grèce ; séminaire tenu au Collège de France,* ed. by Briant, Paris 2001, pp. 81–108.

E. D. COHEN, *The Athenian Nation*, Princeton 2000.

G. COHEN, *The Hellenistic Settlements in Europe, the Islands, and Asia Minor*, Berkeley 1995.

N. CONOVICI, *Histria VIII, Les timbres amphoriques. 2. Sinope*, Bucarest 1998.

IDEM, "Problemes de la chronologie des timbres sinopeens," *Pontica* 30, 1997, pp. 117–154.

G. CORRADI, *Studi Ellenistici*, Torino 1929.

M. CORSARO, "Qualche osservazione sulle procedure di recupero delle terre pubbliche nelle città greche," *Symposion* 1988, edd. by Nenci and Thür, Vienna 1990, pp. 213–229.

CH. COX, "The *Astynomoi,* private Wills and Street Activity," *CQ* 57, 2007, pp. 769–775.

G. DAVERIO ROCCHI, "Topografia dello spazio internazionale. La *hierà hodós* da Atene a Delfi," in *Zu Wasser und zu Land. Verkehrswege in der antiken Welt. Stuttgarter Kolloquium 7, 1999*, edd. by Olshausen and Sonnabend, Stuttgart 2002, pp. 148–159.

N. DESHOURS, *Les Mystères d'Andania: étude d'épigraphie et d'histoire religieuse*, Scripta Antiqua 16, Pessac 2006.

M. DREHER, "Antwort auf F. S. Naiden," in *Symposion* 2007, edd. by Harris and Thür, Vienna 2008, pp. 139–144.

IDEM, "Zu *IG* II² 404, dem athenischen Volkbeschluß über die eigenstaatlichkeit der keischen Poleis," *Symposion* 1985, edd. by Thür, Vienna 1989, pp. 263–281.

H. DUCHÊNE, "La stèle du port. Bilan," *Topoi* 10.1, 2000, pp. 42–46.

IDEM, *La Stèle du port, Fouilles du Port 1. Recherches sur une nouvelle inscription thasienne*, Athens-Paris 1992.

M. ERRINGTON, "König und Stadt im hellenistischen Makedonien: die Rolle des Epistates," *Chiron* 32, 2002, pp. 51–63.

R. ÉTIENNE, *Ténos II. Ténos et les Cyclades du milieu du IVe siècle av. J. C. au milieu du IIIe siècle ap. J. C.*, EFP 1990.

IDEM, "Astu et Polis à Ténos (Cyclades)," *Ktema* 9, 1984, pp. 205–211.

U. FANTASIA, "Aree marginali nella Grecia antica: paludi e bonifiche," in *Demografia, sistemi agrari, regimi alimentari nel mondo antico, Atti del Convegno Internazionale di Studi (Parma 17–19 Ottobre 1997)*, ed. by Vera, Bari 1999, pp. 65–116.

N. F. FEDOSEEV, "Archaeological Evidence on the Athenian Clerouchia," (in Russian), *VDI* 2003.3, pp. 132–140.

IDEM, "Les témoignages archéologiques sur une clérouquie Athénienne a Sinope," *Mouseion* S. III, 2, 2002, pp. 189–202.

P. FERRARESE, "La spedizione di Pericle nel Ponto Eusino," *Contributi dell' istituto di storia antica,* II: *Propaganda e persuasione occulta nell'antichità,* ed. by Sordi, Milan 1974 , pp. 7–19.

CH. FEYEL and R. PROST, "Un règlement délien," *BCH* 122 II, 1998, pp. 455–468.

P. M. FRASER, "Review on Klaffenbach, Die Astynomeninschrift von Pergamon," *JHS* 76, 1956, pp. 138–139.

A. FURTWÄNGLER, "Amphorenfunde in Demetria," in *Demetrias* Band 6, edd. Furtwängler and Zimmer, Würzburg 2003, pp. 119–156.

M. GAGARIN, "The Torture of Slaves in Athenian Law," *CPh* 91.1, 1996, pp. 1–18.

G. GARBRECHT, *Die Wasserversorgung von Pergamon, AvP* I.4, Berlin 2001.

IDEM, "Alimentation en eau de Pergame. Die Entwicklung der Wasserwirtschaft Pergamons bis zur Römischen Kaiserzeit," in *Journées d'Études sur les aqueducts Romains, Tagung über römische Wasserversorgungsanlagen*, Lyon 26–28 Mai 1997, ed. by Garbrecht, Lyon 1999, pp. 141–164.

IDEM, "Die Wasserversorgung des antiken Pergamon," in *L'Eau et les Hommes en Méditerranée et en Mer Noire dans l'antiquité de l'époque mycénienne au règne de Justinien, Actes de congrès international, Athènes, 20–24 mai 1988,* ed. by Gilbert, Athens 1992, pp. 296–318.

IDEM, "Die Wasserversorgung des antiken Pergamon," in *Die Wasserversorgung antiker Städte,* Mainz 1987, pp. 11–48.

IDEM, "Die Madradağ-Wasserleitung von Pergamon," *AW* 9, n. 4, 1978, pp. 40–49.

IDEM, "Fragen der Wasserwirtschaft Pergamons," in *Pergamon: Gesammelte Aufsätze*, Berlin 1972, pp. 43–48.

M. GARCIA MORCILLO, *Las ventas por subasta en el mundo romano: la esfera privada*, Barcelona 2005.

Y. GARLAN, *Les timbres céramiques sinopéens sur amphores et sur tuiles trouvés à Sinope*, Paris 2004.

PH. GAUTHIER, "Epigraphica II," *RPhil.* 67, 1993, pp. 41–55.

IDEM, *Symbola. Les étrangers et la justice dans les cités grecques,* Nancy 1972.

PH. GAUTHIER and M. B. HATZOPOULOS, *La Loi Gymnasiarchique de Beroia*, *Meletemata* 16, Athens 1993.

W. GAWANTKA, *Isopolitie. Ein Beitrag zur Geschichte der zwischenstaatlichen Beziehungen in der griechischen Antike,* Munich 1975.

D. J. GEAGAN, *The Athenian Constitution after Sulla*, *Hesp. Suppl.* 12, Princeton 1967.

H. VAN GELDER, *Geschichte der alten Rhodier*, Haag 1900.

P. GHIONE, *I comuni del regno di Pergamo*, *MRST* serie II, 55, 1905, pp. 67–149.

F. GHINATTI and A. UGUZZONI, *Le tavole greche di Eraclea*, Roma 1968.

A. GIOVANNINI, "Die Tabula Heracleensis: Neue Interpretationen und Perspektiven Teil II: Die lex Iulia municipalis," *Chiron* 38, 2008, pp. 47–61.

V. GIUFFRÈ, "Papiniano: fra tradizione ed innovazione," *ANRW* 15, 1976, pp. 632–666.

F. GSCHNITZER, "Bemerkungen zum Zusammenwirken von Magistraten und Priestern in der griechischen Welt," *Ktema* 14, 1989, pp. 31–38.

E. GRUEN, *The Hellenistic World and the Coming of Rome*, Berkeley 1984.

CH. HABICHT, "Pytheas von Alopeke, Aufseher über die Brunnen Attikas," *ZPE* 77, 1989, pp. 83–87; *corrigenda* 80, 1990, p. 294.

R. Häderli, *Die hellenistischen Astynomen und Agoranomen vornehmlich im alten Athen*, Leipzig 1886.

H. Halfmann, *Städtebau und Bauherren im römischen Kleinasien. Ein Vergleich zwischen Pergamon und Ephesos.* (Istanbuler Mitteilungen Beiheft 43), Tübingen 2001.

K. Hallof, "Ein Dekret aus Kyzikos?," *Asia Minor Studien* 65, 2008, pp. 309–311.

M. Halm-Tisserant, "*XYLA*: de Bois de la Prison, in Carcer, prison et privation de liberté dans l'Antiquité Classique," *Actes du colloque de Strasbourg (5 et 6 décembre 1997)*, Paris 1999, pp. 75–88.

E. V. Hansen, *The Attalids of Pergamon*, Ithaca 1971^2 (1947).

A. Harland, *Associations, Synagoges, and Congregations. Claiming a Place in the Ancient Mediterranean,* Minneapolis 2003.

A. R. W. Harrison, *The Law of Athens,* vols III, Oxford 1968–1971.

K. Harter-Uibopuu, "Hadrian and the Athenian Oil Law," in *Feeding the Ancient Greek City*, edd. by Alston and van Nijf, Leuven 2008, pp. 127–141.

Eadem, "Strafklauseln und gerichtliche Kontrolle in der Mysterieninschrift von Andania," *Dike* 2002, pp. 135–159.

F. W. Hasluck, *Cyzicus*, Cambridge 1910.

R. Heberdey and A. Wilhelm, *Reisen in Kilikien. Denkschriften der Kaiserlischen Akademie der Wissenshaften,* Band 44, Wien 1896.

H. Heinen, "Zur Sklaverei in der hellenistischen Welt (I)," *AncSoc* 7, 1976, pp. 127–149.

M. C. Hellmann, "Caractères de l'épigraphie architecturale de Delphes," in *Delphes cent ans après la Grande fouille. Essai de bilan. Actes du colloque organisé par l'EFA, 17–20 septembre1992*, Ed. by Jacquemin, Athens, *BCH*, Suppl. 36, 2000, pp. 167–177.

Eadem, *Choix d'inscriptions architecturales grecques*, Lyon 1999.

Eadem, *Recherches sur le vocabulaire de l'architecture grecque, d'après lês inscriptions de Délos*, Paris 1992(a).

Eadem, "Le vocabulaire de l'eau dans les inscriptions de Délos," in *L'Eau et les Hommes en Méditerranée et en Mer Noire dans l'antiquité de l'époque mycénienne au règne de Justinien, actes de congrès international, Athènes, 20–24 mai 1988,* ed. by Gilbert, Athens 1992 (b), pp. 181–196.

D. Hennig, "Straßen und Stadtviertel in der griechischen Polis," *Chiron* 30, 2000, pp. 595–615.

Idem, "Staatliche Ansprüche an privaten Immobilienbesitz in der klassischen und hellenistischen Zeit," *Chiron* 25, 1995, pp. 235–282.

P. Herrmann, "Apollon de Pleura: un sanctuaire rural en Lydie entre les Époques Hellénistique et Romaine," in *L' Hellénisme d'Époque Romaine. Noveaux documents, nouvelles approches (I^{er}s. a. C. – IIIes. p. C.)*, ed. by Follet, Paris 2004, pp. 277–286.

H. F. Hitzig, "Astynomeninschrift von Pergamon," *Zeitsch. Der Savigny Stiftung, Rom. Abt.* Bd. 26, 1905, pp. 432–447.

Idem, "Nachtrag zur 'Astynomeninschrift von Pergamon'," *Zeitsch. Der Savigny Stiftung, Rom. Abt.* Bd. 26, 1905, p. 483.

M. Holleaux, *Études d'épigraphie et d'histoire grecque,* Vol. 3, Paris 1942.

W. Hoepfner and E. L. Schwandner, *Haus und Stadt im klassischen Griechenland. Wohnen in der klassischen Polis*, Munich 1986–1994.

J. Hopp, *Untersuchungen zu den letzen Attaliden*, Munich 1977.

N. Jefremow, "Die *aisymnetai* von Sinope," *Klio* 85.1, 2003, pp. 9–14.

C. P. Jones, "Diodorus Pasparos Revised," *Chiron* 30, 2000, pp. 1–14.

Idem, "Diodoros Pasparos and the Nikephoria of Pergamon," *Chiron* 4, 1974, pp. 183–205.

C. Jourdain-Annequin, "Public ou privé ? À propos de quelques cultes d'Héraclès dans la cite grecque," *Ktema* 23, 1998, pp. 354–364.

R. A. Kearsley, "The Milyas and the Attalids: a Decree of the city of Olbasa and a New Royal Letter of the Second Century B. C.," *AS* 44, 1994, pp. 47–57.

B. Keil, "Zu zwei pergamenischen Inschriften," *AM* 29, 1904, pp. 73–78.

G. Klaffenbach, "OPOI ENNAIAΣ," *AM* 76, 1961, pp. 121–126.

Idem, *Varia Epigraphica*, Berlin 1958.

Idem, "Die Astynomeninschrift von Pergamon," *Abhandlung. Berlin Kl. Sprachen Lit.* 6, 1954, pp. 3–25.

E. Klingenberg, "Sull'interdipendenza tra l'agglomerato urbano e il diritto greco," in *La città come fatto di cultura*, Como 1983, pp. 195–213.

Idem, "Die Aufgaben der städtischen Verwaltungsbeamten in Griechenland," *Symposion* 1979, ed. by Dimakis, Vienna 1983, pp. 217–235.

Idem, "La legge platonica sulle fontane pubbliche," *Symposion* 1974, edd. by Modrzejewski and Dimakis, Vienna 1979, pp. 283–305.

D. Knoepfler, "Le contrat d'Érétrie en Eubée pour le drainage de l'étang de Ptéchai," in *Irrigation et drainage dans l'Antiquité, qanāts et canalisations souterraines en Iran, en Egypte et en Grèce ; séminaire tenu au Collège de France,* ed. by Briant, Paris 2001, pp. 41–80.

W. Kolbe, "Die Arbeiten zu Pergamon 1900–1901; Die Astynomeninschrift," *AM* 1902, pp. 47–77.

E. Kosmetatou, "The Attalids of Pergamon," in *A Companion to the Hellenistic World,* ed. by Erskine, Oxford 2003, pp. 154–174.

A. Laronde, *Cyrène et laLybia hellénistique, Lybikai historiai; de l'époque républicaine au principat d'Auguste*, Paris 1987.

K. Latte, *Heiliges Recht. Untersuchungen zur Geschichte der sakralen Rechtsformen in Griechenland*, Tübingen 1920.

S. Lauffer, "Review on Klaffenbach, Die Astynomeinschrift von Pergamon," *HistorZeitsch* 181, 1956, pp. 430–431.

M. Launey, "Le Verger d'Héraklès à Thasos," *BCH* 61, 1937, pp. 380–409.

Cl. Laviosa, "Il santuario di Zeus Megistos e il suo kouros arcaico," in *Studi su Iasos di Caria. Venticinque anni di scavi della Missione archeologica italiana*, BA Suppl. al N° 31–32, 1985, pp. 47–52.

M. Ch. Lécrivain, "La loi des Astynomes de Pergame," *Memoires de L'Academie des Sciences Inscriptions et Belles-Lettres de Toulouse*, II, III 1903, pp. 363–378.

Idem, "Peines et Stipulations du Double et de l'Hémiolion (une fois et demie) dans le Droit Grec," *Memoires de L'Academie des Sciences Inscriptions et Belles-Lettres de Toulouse* 1895, pp. 302–313.

H. Legras, *La Table latine d'Héraclée: la prétendue Lex Iulia Municipalis*, Paris 1907.

D. Lewis, "Keeping Roads clean in Thasos," *CR* 43, 1993, pp. 402–403.

Idem, "The Federal Constitution of Keos," *ABSA* 57, 1962, pp. 1–4.

P. Liddel, "The Places of Publication of Athenian State Decrees from the 5th century to the 3rd century A. D.," *ZPE* 143, 2003, pp. 79–93.

W. Liebeschuetz, "Rubbish Disposal in Greek and Roman Cities," in *Sordes Urbis: la eliminación de residuos en la ciudad romana, Actas de la Reunión de Roma (15–1 de Noviembre de 1996)*, ed. Dupré Raventós, Rome 2000, pp. 51–61.

L. de Ligt and P. W. de Neeve, "Ancient periodic markets. Festivals and fairs," *Athenaeum* 66, 1988, pp. 391–416.

A. LINDENLAUF, *Waste Management in Ancient Greece from the Homeric to the Classical Period: Concepts and Practices of Waste, Dirt, Disposal and Recycling*, PhD Dissertation, University College, London 2000.

H. LOHMANN, "Antike Straßen und Saumpfade in Attika und der Megaris," in *Zu Wasser und zu Land. Verkehrswege in der antiken Welt. Stuttgarter Kolloquium 7, 1999*, edd. by Olshausen and Sonnabend, Stuttgart 2002, pp. 109–147.

Y. LOLOS, "Greek Roads: a commentary on the ancient Terms," *Glotta* 79, 2003, pp. 137–154.

I. LOVE, "A Preliminary Report of the Excavations at Knidos, 1972", *AJA* 77, 4, 1973, pp. 413–424.

E. LUPU, *Greek Sacred Law. A Collection of New Documents (NGSL)*, Leiden 2005.

J. MA, *Antiochos III and the Cities of Western Asia Minor*, Oxford 1999.

D. MACDOWELL, "The Athenian Procedure of Phasis," *Symposion* 1990, ed. by Gagarin, Vienna 1991, pp. 187–198.

IDEM, *The Law in Classical Athens,* London 1978.

D. MAGIE, *Roman Rule in Asia Minor to the end of the Third Century after Christ*, 1950.

A. MAGNETTO, *L'arbitrato di Rodi fra Samo e Priene*, Pisa 2008.

A. MAIURI, *Nuova Silloge epigrafica di Rodi e Cos*, Firenze 1925.

H. MALAY, "New Evidence concerning the Administrative System of the Attalids," *Arkeoloji Dergisi*, 4, 1996, pp. 83–86.

H. MALAY and C. NALBANTOGLU, "The Cult of Apollon Pleurenos in Lydia," *Arkeoloji Dergisi*, 4, 1996, pp. 75–81.

G. MANGANARO, "Affitto di spazi pubblici per le panegyreis ad Akrai," *ZPE* 147, 2004, pp. 115–122.

G. MARTIN, "The Witness's exomosia in Athens," *CQ* 58, 2008, pp. 56–68.

R. MARTIN, "Sur deux expressions techniques de l'architecture grecque," *RPh* 31, 1957, pp. 66–81.

IDEM, *L'Urbanisme dans la Grèce antique*, Paris 1974[2] (1956).

R. MARTINI, "Di una misteriosa operetta attribuita a Papiniano (Norme greche nel Digesto?), forthcoming in the *Atti del XV congresso internazionale dell'Accademia Romanistica Contastiniana*, now in www.ledonline.it/rivistadirittoromano, 2008.

IDEM, "XII Tavole e diritto Greco," *Labeo* 45, 1999, pp. 20–37.

H. J. MASON, *Greek terms for Roman institutions. A Lexicon and Analysis,* Toronto 1974.

H. B. MATTINGLY, "Athens and the Black Sea in the Fifth Century B. C.," in *Sur le traces des Argonautes, actes du 6e symposium de Vani (Colchide) 22–29 septembre 1990*, edd. by Lordkipanidzé and Lévêque, Paris 1996, pp. 151–157.

L. MIGLIARDI ZINGALE, "Ancora sugli *Astynomoi* in D.43.10.1," in *Studi in onore di Remo Martini* II, Milan 2009, pp. 809–819.

G. R. MORROW, *Plato's Cretan City. A Historical Interpretation of the Laws*, Princeton 1960.

H. MÜLLER, "Hadrian an die Pergamener. Eine Fallstudie," in *Selbstdarstellung und Kommunikation*, ed. by Haensch, Munich 2009, pp. 368–406.

IDEM, "Pergamenische Parerga," *Chiron* 33, 2003, pp. 419–445.

IDEM, "Der hellenistische Archiereus," *Chiron* 30, 2000, pp. 519–542.

IDEM, "Hellenistisches Weihnepigramm aus Pergamon," *Chiron* 19, 1989, pp. 499–553.

H. MÜLLER – M. WÖRRLE, "Ein Verein im Hinterland Pergamons zur Zeit Eumenes' II," *Chiron* 32, 2002, pp. 191–235.

G. NACHTERGAEL, "Les Papyrus de la Fondation égyptologique Reine Élisabeth," *ChEg* 47, 1972, pp. 185–203.

P. W. DE NEEVE see L. DE LIGT.

F. S. NAIDEN, "Sanctions in Sacred Laws," in *Symposion* 2007, edd. by Harris and Thür, Vienna 2008, pp. 125–138.

G. NÉMETH, "μεδ' ὄνθον ἐγβαλε͂ν. Regulations concerning everyday life in a Greek Temenos," in *Hekatompedon, Studies in Greek Epigraphy*, Hungarian Polis Studies, Debrecen 1997, pp. 21–30.

R. NEUDECKER, *Die Pracht der Latrine. Zum Wandel öffentlicher Bedürfnisanstalten in der kaiserzeitlichen Stadt,* Munich 1994.

L. NEVETT, "Introduction," in *Ancient Greek Houses and Households*, edd. Ault and Nevett, Philadelphia 2005, pp. 1–11.

EADEM, *House and society in the ancient Greek world*, Cambridge / New York, 1999.

EADEM, "The Organisation of Space in Classical and Hellenistic Houses from mainland Greece and the Western Colonies " in *Time, Tradition and Society in Greek Archaeology: Bridging the "Great Divide"*, ed. Spencer, London 1995, pp. 89–108.

P. M. NIGDELIS, *ΠΟΛΙΤΕΥΜΑ ΚΑΙ ΚΟΙΝΩΝΙΑ ΤΩΝ ΠΟΛΕΩΝ ΤΩΝ ΚΥΚΛΑΔΩΝ ΚΑΤΑ ΤΗΝ ΕΛΛΗΝΙΣΤΙΚΗ ΚΑΙ ΑΥΤΟΚΡΑΤΟΡΙΚΗ ΕΠΟΧΗ*, Thessaloniki 1990.

E. OHLEMUTZ, *Die Kulte und Heiligtümer der Götter in Pergamon,* Würzburg 1968² (1940).

G. J. OLIVER, "Oligarchy at Athens after the Lamian War: epigraphic Evidence for the Boule and the Ekklesia," in *Macedonians in Athens 322–229 B. C.,* edd. by Palagia and Tracy, Exeter 2003, pp. 40–51.

J. H. OLIVER, "The Date of the Pergamene Astynomic Law," *Hesperia* 24, 1955, pp. 88–92.

IDEM, "Review on D. Magie, Roman Rule in Asia Minor to the End of the Third Century after Christ," *AJPh* 72.2, 1951, pp. 198–201.

A. ORLANDOS and I. N. TRAVLOS, *ΛΕΞΙΚΟΝ ΑΡΧΑΙΩΝ ΑΡΧΙΤΕΚΤΟΝΙΚΩΝ ΟΡΩΝ*, Athens 1986.

E. J. OWENS, "The Koprologoi at Athens in the Fifth and Fourth Centuries B. C.," *CQ* 33, 1983, pp. 44–50.

R. PARKER, "What are Sacred Laws?," in *The Law and the Courts in Ancient Greece* edd. by Harris and Rubinstein London 2004, pp. 19–56.

M. PAZ DE HOZ, *Die lydischen Kulte im Lichte der griechischen Inschriften, Asia Minor Studien* 36, Bonn 1999.

D. PEPPAS DELMOUSOU, "Dédicace d'une mesure à grains par deux astynomes (*IG* II² 3939 + 2878) et la politique de l'annone à Athènes sous Auguste," in *L' hellénisme d'époque romaine. Nouveaux documents, nouvelles approches (Ier s. a. C.–IIIe s. p. C.) ; actes du Colloque International à la Mémoire de Louis Robert, Paris, 7–8 juillet 2000,* ed. by Follet, Paris 2004, pp. 121–138.

M. PIÉRART, *Platon et la Cité grecque. Théorie et réalité dans La Constitution des "Lois"*, Bruxelles 2008² (1973).

D. PINKWART and W. STAMMNITZ, *Peristylhäuser Westlich der unteren Agora, AvP* XIV, Berlin 1984.

F. PIRSON, "Pergamon-Bericht über die Arbeiten in der Kampagne 2007," *AA* 2008.2, pp. 88–155.

IDEM, "Pergamon-Bericht über die Arbeiten in der Kampagne 2006," *AA* 2007.2, pp. 13–70.

IDEM, "Pergamon – Das neue Forschungsprogramm und die Arbeiten in der Kampagne 2005," *AA* 2006/2, pp. 55–79.

E. PODDIGHE, *Nel segno di Antipatro. L'eclissi della democrazia ateniese dal 323/2 and 319/8 a. C.*, Rome 2002.

W. K. PRITCHETT, *Studies in Ancient Greek Topography* (Pt. III, Roads), Berkeley 1980.

W. RADT, "The Urban Development of Pergamon," in *Urbanism in Western Asia Minor* ed. by Parrish, Rhode Island 2001, pp. 43–56.

IDEM, *Pergamon, Geschichte und Bauten einer antiken Metropole*, Darmstadt 1999(a).

IDEM, "Pergamon, Vorbericht über die Kampagne 1998," *AA* 1999(b), pp. 291–312.

IDEM, "Recent Research in and about Pergamon," in *Pergamon, Citadel of the Gods*, ed. by Köster, Harrisburg 1998, p. 1–40.

IDEM, "Vorbericht über die Kampagne 1995," *AA* 1996, pp. 443–454.

IDEM, "Landscape and Greek Urban Planning: Exemplified by Pergamon and Priene," in *City and Nature. Changing Relations in Time and Space*, ed. by Christensen, Odense, 1993, pp. 201–210.

IDEM, *Pergamon, Archäologischer Führer*, Istanbul 1989.

W. RAECK, "Neue Forschungen zum spätklassischen und hellenistischen Priene," *Asia Minor Studien* 54, 2005, pp. 147–163.

IDEM, "Das hellenistische Pergamon als Residenzstadt und Polis," *MDAI* (I) 54, 2004, pp. 23–34

G. REGER, "The Mykonian Synoikismos," *REA* 103, 2001, pp. 157–181.

IDEM, "The historical and archaeological Background to the Disappearance of Koresia and Poiessa on Keos," in *Kea-Kythnos: History and Archaeology* edd. by Medoni and Mazarakis, Athens 1998, pp. 633–642.

J. REYNOLDS, *Aphrodisias and Rome*, London 1982.

P. J. RHODES, *A Commentary on the Aristotelian Athenaion Politeia*, Oxford 1981.

K. RIGSBY, *Asylia. Territorial Inviolability in the Hellenistic World*, Berkeley 1996.

L. ROBERT, *Documents d'Asie Mineure*, Paris 1987.

IDEM, "Documents d'Asia Mineure," *BCH* 106, 1982, pp. 309–378.

L. RUBINSTEIN, "'*ARAI*' in Greek Laws in the Classical and Hellenistic Age," in *Symposion* 2005, ed. by Cantarella, Vienna 2007, pp. 269–286.

EADEM, "Volunteer Prosecutor in the Greek World," *Dike* 6, 2003, pp. 87–113.

EADEM, "Main Litigants and Witnesses in the Athenian Courts: Procedural Variations," in *Symposion* 2001, edd. by Wallace and Gagarin, Vienna, 2005, pp. 99–120.

E. RUSCHENBUSCH, *ΣΟΛΩΝΟΣ ΝΟΜΟΙ. Die Fragmente des solonischen Gesetzeswerkes mit einer Text- und Überliferungsgeschichte,* Wiesbaden 1966.

S. SABA, "La Legge degli Astynomoi e la tutela urbanistica a Pergamo nel II secolo a.C.," *Quaderni Lupiensi di Storia e Diritto* I, 2011, pp. 7–32.

EADEM, "Hellenistic Institutions and Law: A Survey (2000–2010)," *Dike* 12/13, 2009/2010, pp. 272–299.

EADEM, "Cisterns in the Astynomoi Law from Pergamon," in *The Nature and Function of Water, Baths, Bathing and Hygiene from Antiquity through the Renaissance*, edd. by Kosso and Scott, Leiden 2009, pp. 149–162.

EADEM, "Ἄμφοδα in Hellenistic Times: Urban Planning and philological Interpretation," *AntCl.* 77, 2008, pp. 79–90.

C. SALIOU, *Les lois des Bâtiments. Voisinage et habitat urbain dans l'Empire Romaine. Recherches sur les rapports entre le droit et la construction privée du siècle d'Auguste au siècle de Justinien*, Beirut 1994.

F. SARTORI, "Eraclea di Lucania," *Röm. Mitt.*, Suppl. XI, 1967.

IDEM, "Società e diritto nelle tavole greche di Eraclea," *Atene e Roma* 10, 4, 1965, pp. 145–160.

I. SAVALLI-LESTRADE, "Les Attalides et les cités grecque d'Asia Mineure au IIe siècle a.C.," in *Les cites d'Asia Mineure occidentale au IIe siècle a.C.*, edd. by Bresson and Descat, Bordeaux 2001(a), pp. 77–91.

EADEM, "Amici del re, alti funzionari e gestione del potere principalmente nell'Asia Minore ellenistica," *Simblos* 3, 2001(b), pp. 263–294.

EADEM, *Les Philoi Royaux dans l'Asie Héllenistique*, Geneva 1998.

W. SCHEIDEL, "Population and Demography," in *A Companion to Ancient History* ed. by Erskine, London 2009, pp. 134–145.

E. SCHWEIZER, *Grammatik der pergamenischen Inschriften. Beiträge zur Laut- und Flexionslehre der gemeingriechischen Sprache*, Berlin 1898.

J. SEYFARTH, "Φράτρα und Φρατρία im nachklassischen Griechentum," *Aegyptus* 35, 1955, pp. 3–38.

B. SHERK, "The Eponymous Officials of Greek Cities IV," *ZPE* 93, 1992, pp. 223–272.

J. SOSIN, "Unwelcome Dedications: Public Law and Private Religion in Hellenistic Laodicea by the Sea," *CQ* 55.1, 2005, pp. 130–139.

IDEM, "Half again more," *ArchPF* 50, 2004, pp. 40–44.

W. STAMMNITZ see D. PINKWART.

P. STANLEY, *Ancient Greek Markets Regulations and Controls*, Berkeley Diss. 1976.

R. STROUD, *The Athenian Grain-Tax Law of 374/3 B. C., Hesperia Suppl.* Vol. 29, Princeton 1998.

G. THÜR, "Response to Lene Rubinstein," in *Symposion* 2001, edd. by Wallance and Gagarin, Vienna 2005, pp. 121–124.

IDEM, "Bemerkungen zum altgriechischen Werkvertrag," in *Studi in Onore di Arnaldo Biscardi* V, Milano 1984, pp. 471–514.

M. TRÜMPER, *Die ‚Agora des Italiens' in Delos,* Rahden/Westf. 2008.

C. TRÜMPY, *Untersuchungen zu den altgriechischen Monatsnamen und Monatsfolgen*, Heildeberg 1997.

A. UGUZZONI see A. GHINATTI 1968.

R. VALLOIS, "*ARAI*," *BCH* 38, 1914, pp. 250–271.

CL. VATIN, see F. SALVIAT

IDEM, "Jardins et services de voire," *BCH* 100, 1976, pp. 555–564.

C. VIAL, *Délos indépendante (314–167 av. J.-C.). Étude d'une communauté civique et de ses institutions, BCH* Suppl. X. 1985.

B. VIRGILIO, "La città ellenistica e i suoi benefattori: Pergamo e Diodoro Pasparos," *Athenaeum* 82, 1994, pp. 299–314.

IDEM, *Gli Attalidi di Pergamo. Fama, Eredità, Memoria. Studi Ellenistici* V, Pisa 1993.

IDEM, "Strabone e la storia di Pergamo e degli Attalidi," in *Studi Ellenistici I*, Pisa 1984, pp. 24–37.

A. V. WALSER, "Sympolitien und Siedlungsentwicklung," in *Stadtbilder im Hellenismus. Die hellenistische Polis als Lebensform* Bd. 1, edd. by Matthaei and Zimmermann, Berlin 2009, pp. 135–155.

A. WILHELM see under HEBERDEY 1896.

G. WOODHEAD, "Review on Klaffenbach, Die Astynomeninschrift von Pergamon," *CR* 70, 1956, pp. 79–80.

M. WÖRRLE, see MÜLLER 2002.

IDEM, "Pergamon um 133 v.Chr.," *Chiron* 30, 2000, pp. 542–576.

IDEM, "Wasserrecht und -verwaltung in griechischer Zeit," Mitteilungen, Leichweiss-Institut für Wasserbau der Technischen Universität Braunschweig, 1981 pp. 71–97.

IDEM, "Die Lex Sacra von dem Asklepieion," *AvP* VIII.3, Berlin 1969.

U. WULF, *Die Stadtgrabung. Die hellenistischen und romischen Wohnhauser von Pergamon unter besonderer Berucksichtigung der Anlage zwischen der Mittel- und der Ostgasse in der Stadtgrabung von Pergamon*, *AvP* XV.3, Berlin 1999.

EADEM, "The Hellenistic and Roman Houses of Pergamon," in *Pergamon, Citadel of the Gods*, ed. by Köster, Harrisburg 1998, pp. 299– 330.

EADEM, "Der Stadtplan von Pergamon," *IstMitt* 44, 1994, pp. 135–175.

A. ZACCARIA-RUGGIU, "L'intervento pubblico nella regolamentazione dello spazio privato. Problemi giuridici," *Rivista di archeologia* 14, 1990, pp. 77–94.

G. ZUCHTRIEGEL, "Öffentliche Latrinen in der Astynomeninschrift von Pergamon," *ZPE* 167, 2008, pp. 85–87.

11 Indices

Ancient Literary Sources

Index of Inscriptions

Index of Papyri

General Index

(Topics already mentioned in the TOC are not listed in the general index.)

Selected Greek and Latin Words

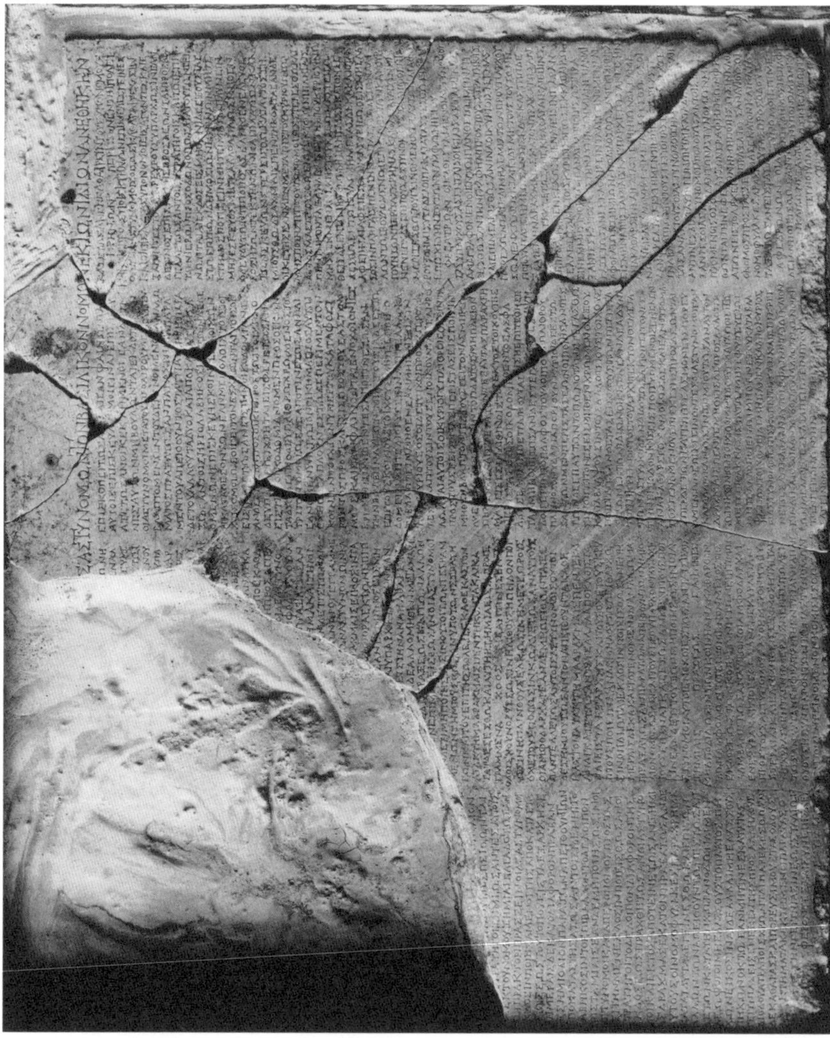

Fig. 1: Picture of the Astynomoi Law provided by H. Müller. Courtesy of the DAI Munich.

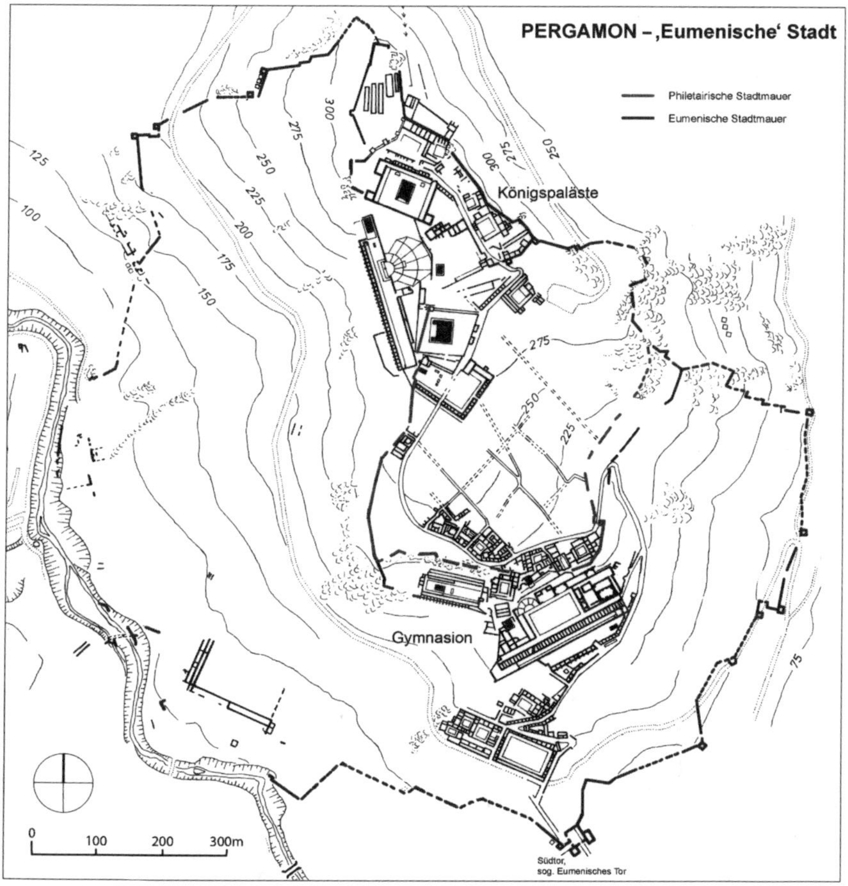

Fig. 2: Map of Roman Pergamon from F. Pirson, "Stadtraum und Städtebau im hellenistischen Pergamon," in *Pergamon. Panorama der antiken Metropole*, Berlin 2011, pp. 66–73. Courtesy of the Pergamon Excavation, DAI Istanbul.